Start to Stitch

Nancy Nicholson,
Claire Buckley
and
Miriam Edwards

SEARCH PRESS

First published in Great Britain 2013
Search Press Ltd
Wellwood
North Farm Road
Tunbridge Wells
Kent TN2 3DR

Based on the following books published by Search Press:
Start to Appliqué by Nancy Nicholson, 2008
Start to Embroider by Claire Buckley, 2008
Start to Patchwork by Nancy Nicholson, 2009
Start to Quilt by Miriam Edwards, 2008

Text copyright © Nancy Nicholson, Claire Buckley and Miriam Edwards 2013

Photographs by Debbie Patterson at Search Press Studios and by Roddy Paine Photographic Studios

Photographs and design copyright © Search Press Ltd 2013

ISBN: 978-1-84448-907-7

The Publishers and authors can accept no responsibility for any consequences arising from the information, advice or instructions given in this publication.

Suppliers
If you have difficulty obtaining any of the materials and equipment mentioned in this book, please visit the Search Press website: www.searchpress.com

Some words are underlined <u>like this</u>. They are explained in the glossary on page 175.

The publishers would like to thank consultant Rebecca Vickers and also the following for appearing in the photographs: Georgia Brooks, Emily Murayama, Ellie and Catriona Outram, Henrietta Amos, Josie Paine, Beth Miller, Jade Searles, Joelle Nicholson, Nicola Fields, Catherine Stevens, Yuna Murayama, Amanda Abrahim, Katherine Chandrain, Chloe Barnard, Rebekah Mate-Kole Rampe, Charlie de la Bédoyère, Katrina Hindley, Charlotte Brooks, Phoebe Cheong, Lucia Brisefer and Abby Jeffery.
Thanks also to Sandy Paine and to Ozzy and Daisy.

Printed in Malaysia

Contents

Introduction

The four crafts in this book – <u>appliqué</u>, <u>embroidery</u>, <u>patchwork</u> and <u>quilting</u> – are known and loved worldwide, with histories stretching back thousands of years. There is a wealth of inspiration to draw upon! All four crafts involve decorating fabrics, or using fabrics as decorations themselves.

Appliqué is the craft of adding decorative fabrics to background fabrics, and is used by many textile artists today. You can use appliqué techniques to decorate your clothes and home furnishings.

Embroidery is embellishing and decorating fabrics with stitches, beads, sequins and other fabrics – in other words, combining all those choice sparkling bits in your cupboard with richly coloured and patterned cloth.

Patchwork is a great way to recycle old clothes, or use up loose scraps of materials from other craft projects. Get started right away by asking your friends and family for their old clothes for you to work some magic upon. You will be surprised how beautiful something made from reused materials can be, so even when your favourite pair of jeans wears through, they can live on as a brand new bag, or belt, or quilt!

Quilting is the craft of combining layers of fabric, trapping padding between a backing and a decorative top fabric. This 'quilt sandwich' makes a warm and cosy fabric that is then joined with stitches or with ties, buttons or beads. Like the other crafts, quilting is as versatile and creative as the artist; find inspiration in lovely colourful fabrics and textures and lose yourself in the craft.

In this book you will find lots of simple projects, and once you have mastered the basic techniques, you will be able to start inventing other uses for these versatile crafts – creativity breeds inspiration, so the more you do, the more you will find yourself wanting to do. Good luck!

Materials

Surface fabrics

Many fabrics come striped, spotted, dyed in different colours, or printed with designs, so there will always be a fabric that you like. Always wash and iron your fabric before using it. This takes out all the chemicals, and if the colour is going to run it is better to find out now.

Choose colours and fabrics you would like to work with, as you will spend time and energy on your project and you want to look at it with love and pride. When you are more experienced, you can experiment with all kinds of fabric.

The best fabrics to use for appliqué are crisp cottons. They come in various weights, from dress fabrics to heavier furnishing cottons, which are useful for cushion backs and bags. There are companies that sell 'fat quarters' for patchworkers. These are usually 45.7 x 56cm (18 x 22in), and are ideal for appliqué in both size and weight and not too expensive. Some bright pieces of felt can be useful and attractive.

TOP TIP!

If you choose a fabric but the colour runs when you wash it, put a handful of cooking salt in the rinse water. Soak it for half an hour, then rinse it. Pat it with a white cloth. If it still loses colour, choose another fabric!

A selection of crisp cotton fabrics and bias binding in several colours, suitable for all the projects.

You can use many different fabrics in your embroidery. These include cotton, felt and denim, as well as more unusual fabrics like calico, a firm woven cotton fabric which can be bought unbleached or bleached white; cotton lawn, a very soft, finely woven cotton fabric; organza, a thin, stiff and translucent woven fabric which can be made from silk or synthetic fibres; net, an open mesh fabric used in layers over other fabrics to add colour and strength; and brocade, a rich fabric often made of silk woven with a raised pattern.

For patchwork, you can use any scraps of dressmaking-quality fabrics for most of the projects, though cotton is always best. Try to use the same weight of fabric for each individual project, as it will go together much more evenly and give a better finish.

For ease, you should use 100 per cent cotton for quilting as it does not fray and slip like other fabrics. For some projects you will want to quilt around shapes or patterns on the top fabric, so choose one with a good design. As with appliqué, felt can be fun for decorating quilted projects.

In shadow quilting, the design is attached to the background fabric and a lightweight, transparent fabric is placed on top. You then stitch round the design, attaching the layers together. I have used a sheer fabric called voile for the top fabric but you can also use net.

Felt is used in some of the projects.

Wadding and supporting fabrics

Wadding Low loft polyester wadding is used for the padding layer of quilt projects. You can also use a cotton mix of eighty per cent cotton and twenty per cent polyester (80/20) for the quilted Cat Wall Hanging on pages 164–173 because it is flatter. Wadding is called 'batting' in the US.

Bias binding This is a narrow strip of fabric that comes in many colours. It is used in embroidery to wrap around the inner ring of a tambour ring to protect the fabric when it is pulled tight. It can also be used for a quick and simple edging in the appliquéd Felt Bag project on pages 46–51 and the patchwork Pet's Blanket on pages 98–103.

Sewing equipment

Sewing machine Some of the projects require a sewing machine, but you do not need an elaborate one. For most of the projects, it needs only to be able to do straight stitch and zigzag stitch. The patchwork Heart Decoration on pages 118–123 uses a heart-shaped machine embroidery stitch, but if your machine will not do this, you could embroider the piece by hand instead.

Pins Glass-headed pins or ordinary sewing pins can be used. If you can get some longer pins, they are useful for pinning layers of quilt together. A thimble and sewing cushion are very handy.

Glass-headed pins and needles in a pin cushion, sewing scissors and smaller sharp scissors, stranded embroidery threads and sewing threads in many colours.

Scissors Use embroidery scissors to cut threads, cords and ribbons., a large sharp pair for cutting fabric, and pinking shears where you want a fancy edge. Do not use your fabric scissors for cutting paper or card. For cutting florist wire, use a pair of old scissors.

Needles Buy a packet of mixed needles so that you can find one that is right for you. For quilting, choose fine, long pins that you can see easily. Fine pins will not damage your fabric. You may find a big eye no. 10 needle useful. This is a small needle, so it helps make small stitches, but it has a big eye, which makes it easy to thread. For bigger stitches or thicker thread, use an embroidery needle, a no. 7 with a sharp point.

For embroidery you need to have a needle with a long eye so that the thread goes into the eye easily. Tapestry needles are very large, and used for embroidering with thick threads. They are also known as ballpoint needles.

A beading needle has a very fine eye so that you can be sure it will fit through the hole in the bead. Needles for patchwork tend to be shorter, but a pack of assorted sewing needles will be fine. Use a pin cushion to keep pins safe, and a thimble to protect your fingers when sewing.

Threads

Stranded embroidery thread This type of thread (called six-strand embroidery floss in the US) is used for most embroidery, and is made up of six thin strands. It is bought in a skein, and the thread is usually pulled apart into three strands before you start to embroider. It is a good idea to buy a selection of colours so that you have a variety to suit whichever project you are doing. The good thing about stranded threads is that you can choose the number of strands for the thickness you need.

Perlé cotton thread In addition to stranded embroidery thread, you can use perlé cotton thread (called pearl cotton in the US). This comes in a ball and is twisted together, meaning that you do not need to split the thread before embroidering. You can also use metallic threads, which are useful to couch on to a fabric (see page 60) or for handles and decorations.

Sewing threads You will also need a range of coloured sewing threads to use in your sewing machine. Some projects need the machine stitching to match the colour fabric you have chosen. You will also need ordinary sewing thread for tacking.

Quilting thread This is a special type of thread used for quilting. It is cotton wrapped in polyester and comes in a rainbow of colours, either to match your work or to contrast.

Other threads For decorative stitches, use coton à broder or perlé, or thicker threads if you really want the stitches to show up. Some decorative threads are sold in mixed bags of threads in different textures that blend in beautifully together. Thick, variegated thread and variegated crochet cotton are used in many of the projects.

Pinking shears.

FUNKY FACT!
Many people collect equipment used for embroidery. Sometimes really old pieces can be rare and valuable.

TOP TIP!
To keep your equipment together and ready to use, store your pieces safely in a sewing box or basket.

Embellishments

Beads Glass, metal or plastic shapes with a hole through the centre. Thread is passed through the hole to secure the bead to the fabric. You will need a selection of seed beads which you can buy in a wonderful array of colours. You may want to buy some slightly bigger beads too, if you think they will suit your project.

Sequins Small shiny shapes that can be sewn on to fabric for decoration. These can be bought in a great variety of shapes, sizes and colours in craft or fabric stores.

Craft jewels These are shiny plastic shapes that look like real jewels, and are used for decorating your embroidery.

Buttons These make good decorations, as well as being useful to secure bags. You can buy a selection of buttons at good fabric stores, or ask your friends and family if they have a 'button box' for odd buttons.

Ribbons You will need fine satin and organza ribbon for the projects in this book, from 3–5mm (1/8–¼in) wide. Choose ribbons to complement the colour of your chosen fabrics.

Pompoms Sold on a braid, these are used to trim cushions and curtains.

Imitation suede lacing This can be found in fabric stores or craft shops.

Chocolate wrappers These are used in the embroidered Funky Book Cover project (see pages 72–77) for decoration.

Florist wire This is used for making flower arrangements, but it is really useful for all kinds of crafts. You can buy it in florist's shops. Turquoise florist wire is used to make fun spirals for the quilted Cat Wall Hanging (see pages 164–173).

Beaded trim These are great for finishing off projects. I used a green one to decorate a book cover that goes with the quilted Notebook Cover project (see pages 140–143).

Sheesha These are small mirrors that are sewn on to a fabric.
Sheesha are used a lot in Indian embroidery.

Pompoms, ribbons and buttons.

Sequins, seed beads, craft jewels and mock sheesha.

Other materials

Iron You will need an iron set to medium to hot when you are using fusible web. Always make sure you have an adult around when using a hot iron.

Fusible web This is a fine webbing of heat-activated material with a paper backing, used to fuse together two pieces of fabric. The paper side of the webbing is ironed to the reverse of the fabric. Then the template is drawn around and the shape cut out. After removing the backing paper the shape can be positioned and ironed into place.

Kapok filling Kapok filling or similar stuffing can be bought from a craft store.

Ballpoint pen and **soft pencil** These are used for drawing your patterns on to paper and card.

Press studs These are known as 'snaps' in the USA, and need to be at least 5mm (¼in) wide.

Brooch back This is used in the Brilliant Brooch project on pages 18–21.

Cushion pad This is known as a 'pillow form' in the USA. You will need a 36 x 36cm (14¼ x 14¼in) cushion pad for the Throw Cushion project on pages 34–39.

Washable felt pens These are ideal for drawing on fabric because they wash out.

Permanent marker You can use this to draw on felt or other fabrics.

Chalk markers These are useful for marking dark fabrics, as in the Sashiko Bag project (see pages 152–157). The chalk brushes off later.

Tape measure and **ruler** These are used to measure fabric and embellishments.

Safety pins These are used to keep your quilt sandwich together while you work on it.

Fabric adhesive spray This is used to stick the layers of quilt sandwich together before quilting. It should be used in a well-ventilated room. Read the instructions carefully.

Sticky tape This is used to tape down patterns.

Compasses These are used for drawing circles.

Notebook You make a cover for this in the Notebook Cover project on pages 140–143.

Bag handles These are used in the Sashiko Bag project on pages 152–157.

Dowelling This is used for the Cat Wall Hanging on pages 164–173.

Plastic, card and brown paper for templates Ordinary brown parcel paper is useful for cutting out patterns. Where you need to make a stronger template, you can photocopy the patterns from the book, cut them out and draw round them on card. You can also trace patterns on to an old transparent plastic folder and cut them out.

Craft interfacing You can buy this in fabric stores. It comes in different weights, some for a stiffer effect, some lighter. It is used in the projects to stiffen the fabric. Ensure that you iron with the rough side down on the wrong side of the fabric you are using.

Tambour ring A tambour ring (also known as an embroidery ring; or an embroidery hoop in the US) is used to hold fabric tight for embroidering.

Glue stick This is used to hold chocolate wrappers in place before they are stitched on securely in the Funky Book Cover project on pages 72–77.

Safety pins These metal pins can be fixed to the end of a ribbon to pull it through a drawstring bag.

Above: paper and brown paper, press studs, kapok filling, pencil, pen, cushion pad, brooch back, glue stick.

Below: fabric adhesive spray, sticky tape, an iron, a notebook, compasses, a chalk marker, washable pens, a pencil and permanent marker, dowelling, safety pins, old scissors, bag handles, fusible web, a press stud, tape measure, ruler and card.

APPLIQUÉ

Nancy Nicholson

Appliqué means to apply one smaller piece of fabric or decorative element to a background of fabric. When you wear out your jeans, and stitch a patch over the tear, this is appliqué!

Appliqué has been used throughout history to decorate clothes and home furnishings in countries all around the world. Whenever fabric was scarce, pieces of fabric were cut from old materials and sewn on to newer cloth to decorate it. Perhaps the earliest example is an Egyptian canopy of appliquéd leather dating from 980 BC. The best known use of appliqué is in the quilts produced from the 1600s to the present day in the USA and Europe. Visit museums and craft galleries to see appliqué from around the world.

Appliqué offers a wide range of creative possibilities and is used by many textile artists today. You can find clothing and household items decorated with appliqué and embroidery in many stores, and it is well worth looking around for ideas to try.

My very first introduction to sewing was sitting next to my mother watching her making dolls clothes for me. When I was old enough, she would give me scraps of material and beads and thread to experiment on my own.

I came to appliqué when my children were very small. The first items I made were little bibs, with animals and birds on them. I progressed to making quilts and wanted to add a very individual touch to the plain, bright colours I was using. So after designing some simple animal and bird shapes I applied them to the patchwork squares, making them very much more personal. I then began making appliquéd pictures using unusual fabrics, and layered pieces using silks and velvets, and covered in layers of hand and machine embroidery. I am continuously finding new and exciting ways to use appliqué in the projects I design, and just love the seemingly endless possibilities!

In this book you will find lots of easy projects, and once you have mastered the basic techniques, you will be able to start inventing other uses for this versatile craft. Many of the projects in the section can be made to give as a special handmade gift, to friends or family.

Appliqué techniques

Using fusible web

This is an easy way to attach the appliqué shapes to your background, ensuring that they are held in place while you apply decorative stitches, either by machine or hand sewing.

STAY SAFE

Always have an adult with you when you are ironing.

1 Place the fusible web sticky side down on the fabric and iron it on a hot setting.

2 Draw round your template with a pencil.

3 Cut out the shape.

4 Peel the backing paper off the fusible web.

5 Put the shape sticky side down on the backing fabric and iron it on using a hot setting.

The shape will now be firmly fixed on to your backing fabric.

Machine stitching

You can use a sewing machine to sew a seam, as shown below. You can also use it to sew on shapes instead of using fusible web or hand stitching.

STAY SAFE

Always ask an adult to help you set up the sewing machine.

1 Line up your fabric carefully. Use the gauge to set a 1cm (⅜in) <u>seam allowance</u> and lower the machine's foot.

2 Set the machine to the stitch you want. This is running stitch. Press the foot pedal to sew.

3 When you have finished sewing, lift up the foot, slide out the sewn fabric and snip the threads.

Hand stitching

Starting and finishing running stitch

1 Thread your needle. Knot the end of the thread and bring the needle up from the back to the front of the fabric.

2 Take the needle down and then up and down again to make two evenly sized stitches.

3 Pull the thread through. Now you can see the stitches.

4 Continue sewing to make a row of stitches.

5 You now need to fasten off the stitching. At the back of the fabric, take the needle through the last stitch you made from right to left. Pull the thread through and repeat.

6 Take the needle through from right to left again, but do not pull it tight, leave a loop and take the needle through the loop.

7 Pull the thread through to make a knot and trim with scissors.

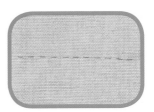

A finished row of running stitch.

TOP TIP!
Fasten off all your stitching in this way, not just running stitch.

Slip stitch appliqué

1 Thread the needle, knot the end and come up from the back of the backing fabric. Go through the edge of the shape.

2 Pull through and stitch through the backing fabric and the edge of the shape again.

3 Continue stitching right round the shape and fasten off at the back in the same way as for running stitch.

The finished appliquéd shape.

Closed fly stitch

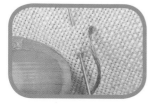

1 Thread the needle and knot the end. Come up from the back and go down to make the first stitch, which is a kind of stalk. Bring the needle up again diagonally to the left.

2 Pull through. You can now see the stalk stitch. Make a loop round to the right and hold it down with your thumb. Go down to the top right of the stalk and bring the needle up at the bottom of the stalk. Pull through to reveal the stitch.

3 Come up at the top of the next stalk stitch to continue. When you have finished stitching, go down at the end and fasten off as before.

A finished row of closed fly stitch.

Star stitch

1 Knot the end, come up from the back, make a straight stitch and go down.

2 Pull through. Find the middle of the first stitch. Come up to one side of it and go down on the other side to complete a cross shape.

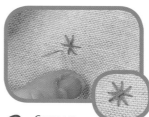

3 Come up between the two bars of the cross to make a diagonal stitch across it. Come up again to start another diagonal stitch, and go down on the other side of the cross to complete the star shape.

Finished star stitches.

Sewing on beads

1 Use a fine needle that will go through the bead's hole. Come up from the back. Pick up a bead on your needle and push it to the bottom of the thread.

2 Go down close to where you came up and come up ready to sew on the next bead.

3 Pick up another bead and continue as before.

A row of beads.

Sewing on sequins with beads

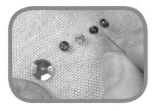
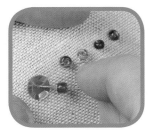

I Knot the thread, come up from the back and pick up a sequin on your needle.

2 Pick up a bead as well, then go down through the same hole in the centre of the sequin. The bead will trap your sequin in place. When you have finished attaching sequins, fasten off at the back.

A row of sequins and beads.

Sewing on buttons

I Thread the needle with doubled thread and knot the end. Come up through one of the central holes in the button and go down through the other one.

2 Repeat four times and fasten off at the back.

Ladder stitch

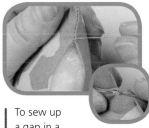

I To sew up a gap in a piece, come up through the machine stitching to hide the knot inside the piece. Make a small stitch along the fold on one side of the gap.

2 Pull through and make another small stitch along the fold on the other side of the gap.

3 Continue until the whole gap is sewn up. To fasten off, go back under the machine stitching and up again.

4 Repeat several times and trim.

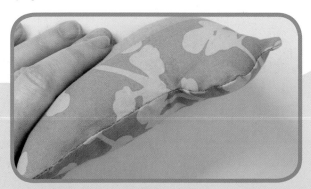

The finished stitching is very hard to see.

Brilliant Brooch

This brooch is made using brightly coloured felt and sparkling seed beads, and it would make any plain coat look individual and unusual. Try making brooches in different shapes and design your own motifs.

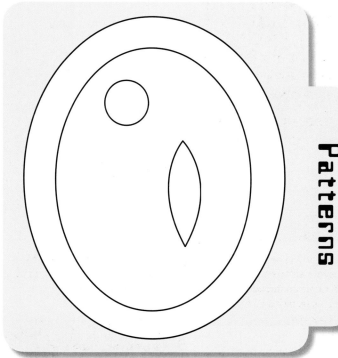

Patterns

The patterns for the brooch and its appliqué decorations, shown full size.

! STAY SAFE
Always have an adult with you when you are ironing.

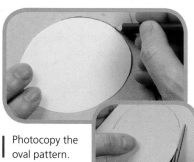

1 Photocopy the oval pattern. Cut out the oval shape and draw round it on a piece of card. Cut out the card oval to make a template.

2 Apply fusible web to pale blue and bright pink scraps of felt (see page 14). Make leaf and circle templates. Draw round the circle seven times on the fusible web on the bright pink felt. Draw round the leaf template eight times on the fusible web on the pale blue felt.

3 Apply fusible web to deep pink and orange felt scraps. Cut the scraps into strips 6mm (¼in) wide. Peel off the backing of the fusible web and cut the strips into three deep pink and four orange squares.

4 Make a template from the larger oval pattern, draw round it on green felt and cut out two oval shapes.

5 Peel off the backing from the pale blue felt leaves. Arrange the leaves in a circle, starting at the centre of one of the green felt ovals. Iron them on.

6 Thread a needle with one strand of bright pink embroidery thread. Knot the end. Make one long stitch in the centre of a leaf, then come up to the left of it. Go down at the base of the first central stitch, and come up to the right of it to make a second diagonal stitch.

7 Peel off the backing from the circles. Place them in the centre of the brooch with the squares on top as shown. Iron them on, pressing firmly.

8 Thread a beading needle or fine-eyed needle with pink thread and knot the end. Come up through the centre of the square, pick up a green bead and go back down.

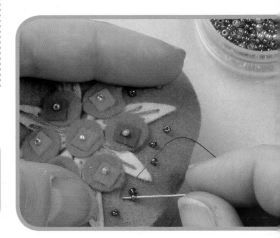

9 Complete all the squares, then sew three pink beads in each of the gaps between the leaves.

TOP TIP!

When ironing on using fusible web, make sure the glue side is down.

TOP TIP!

Keep seed beads in a saucer or little dish when you are sewing them on, to stop them rolling away.

10 Thread a needle and sew round the edge of each oval in long running stitches, 4mm (³⁄₁₆in) from the edge. Do not trim the tail of the thread.

11 Make two card templates from the smaller oval pattern. Put kapok filling in the decorated felt oval.

12 Put one small oval template on top of the kapok filling. Pull the tail of thread from the running stitches to gather the edges of the oval. With the thread pulled tight, make several stitches to secure the gathering.

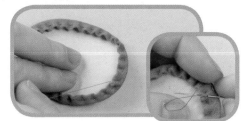

19

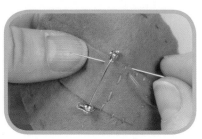

13 Cut a 1.5cm x 3cm (⅝ x 1¼in) piece of the same green felt. Attach fusible web to it as shown on page 14 and peel off the backing. Thread the piece fusible web side down through the brooch back and iron it on to the second felt oval.

14 Thread a needle with doubled green thread and use straight stitches to sew the felt rectangle on to the oval to secure the brooch back.

15 Place the second small oval template in the centre of the felt oval on the other side from the brooch back. Pull the thread to gather the edges and secure with stitches as in step 12.

16 Thread a needle with two strands of embroidery thread and knot the end. Bring the needle up to hide the knot under the felt overlap of the decorated oval as shown.

17 Place the two ovals wrong sides together and sew them together using ladder stitch as shown on page 17.

What next?

Try using different colour schemes, motifs and decorative stitches to brighten up your brooches. They make great gifts for family and friends!

21

Skirt Trim

All through the centuries people have used appliqué to decorate their clothes, using ribbons, buttons and all manner of fabrics. Here is a way to decorate any piece of clothing, but it looks especially good on a flowing skirt. Once you have done this simple project, try making the design a little more elaborate by adding more flowers.

You will need

Skirt to decorate

Card, pencil and scissors

Scraps of three different fabrics

Needle and sewing thread and embroidery threads to match and contrast with fabrics

Enough organza ribbon to trim round whole skirt hem

Pins

Buttons

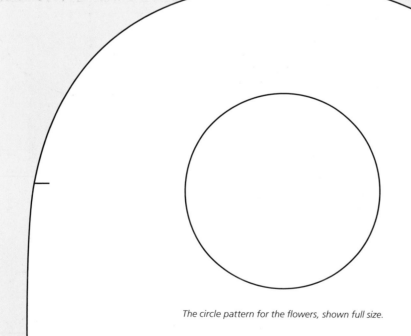

Patterns

The circle pattern for the flowers, shown full size.

The arch pattern for the Skirt Trim, shown full size.

2 Make a card template from the circle in the same way. Draw round the template on your fabric scraps and cut out the circles.

1 Photocopy the arch pattern. Cut out the shape and draw round it on a piece of card. Cut out the card shape to make a template. Make the two little marks in the sides. Place the flat edge of the card template along the hem of your chosen skirt. Draw round the rounded part of the shape up to the little marks. Repeat all round the skirt.

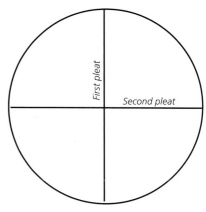

3 Use your fingers to make a pleat in one of the fabric circles.

4 Thread a needle and make a couple of stitches in the centre of the circle to hold the pleat in place.

First pleat

Second pleat

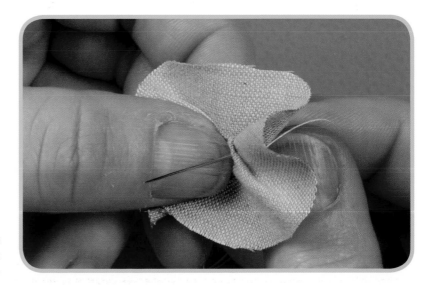

5 Turn the circle round and make the second pleat. Stitch it in place and fasten off securely.

6 Cut the organza ribbon into lengths of 21cm (8¼in). Place one length over one of your pencil lines, making sure the line is in the centre of the ribbon. Pin the ribbon in place.

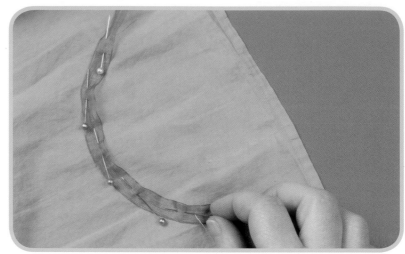

TOP TIP!

Always pin and tack your work first to make the final sewing easier.

7 Tack the ribbon in place with long running stitches. Use contrasting thread to running stitch round the semi-circle. Here I have used red embroidery thread. Do not trim the thread at the end of the semi-circle.

8 Place a flower and a button on the end of the semi-circle of ribbon and use the tail end of the thread to sew them on as shown.

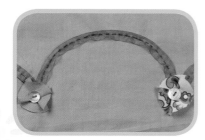

The finished skirt hem.

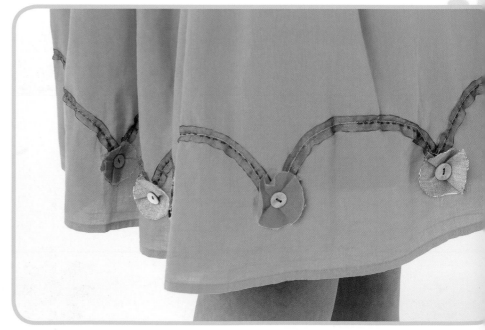

What next?

Try sewing flowers on to your jeans. You can make the flowers bigger or use several layers. It also looks good if you cut out the flowers with pinking shears.

Perfect Picture

Hand appliqué can be used in many different ways to make pictures like this one or unique cards and gifts. You can use the same technique to apply fabric to clothes, quilts or cushions. Once you have made this simple picture, you will be able to create your own designs.

The patterns for the Perfect Picture, shown full size. You will need to make card templates for the larger and the smaller shapes.

Patterns

26

1 Make a card template from the larger leaf pattern and draw round it on a scrap of purple fabric.

2 Cut out the leaf shape.

3 Thread a needle and sew round the shape 4mm (³/₁₆in) from the edge, in running stitch. Do not trim the end as you are going to use it for gathering.

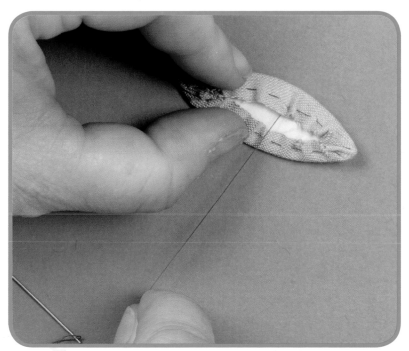

4 Make a card template from the smaller leaf shape. Place this in the centre of the fabric leaf and pull the tail of the thread to gather the edges.

 STAY SAFE
Always have an adult with you when you are ironing.

5 Iron both sides of the leaf shape.

  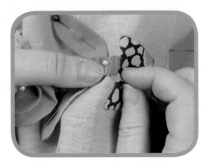

6 Do a couple of stitches to secure the gathering thread, then trim it. Take out the card template. Follow steps 1 to 6 for all the other shapes: the two flower circles and the heart, the flower pot and stalk and the other leaf. Use a variety of fabrics as shown.

7 Pin all the pieces in place on your backing fabric.

8 Slip stitch all the pieces in place (see page 15). Use matching thread for each piece.

9 Decorate the leaves with closed fly stitch as shown on page 16. Sew round the flower and the heart with running stitch and decorate the background with star stitch (see page 16). Sew a button on the flower pot (see page 17).

TOP TIP!

When sewing shapes on to backing fabric, do not pull the stitches too tight.

The finished picture in a frame.

What next?

Any simple drawing can be used for an appliqué picture. The fabric and stitching will create the detail, so the simpler the design the better!

Beady Bird

Appliquéd stuffed toys and hanging decorations have been made for hundreds of years. This bird is simple to make and once you have mastered one, you could make a whole family of them, all decorated in different ways. They make lovely Christmas decorations, or can be filled with lavender to make a sweet-smelling gift.

You will need

Card, pencil and scissors

Cream backing fabric

Fabric scraps in five plain colours, and fusible web to cover

Iron

Six sequins and six beads

Embroidery threads to contrast with fabrics

Pins and thread for tacking

Sewing machine with cream sewing thread

Kapok filling

Ribbon, 24cm (9½in) and button

Patterns

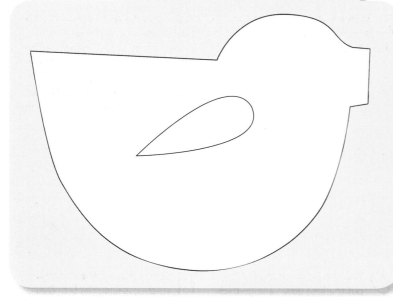

The patterns for the bird and the petal shape, shown half size. Enlarge them to 200% on a photocopier, then make card templates of them.

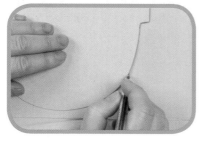

1 Enlarge the patterns on a photocopier and cut out the bird. Draw round it on card to make a template. Draw round the template on your backing fabric.

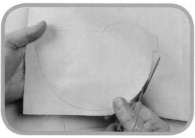

2 Cut out the shape. Repeat to make the other side of the bird.

3 Apply fusible web to the five fabric scraps. Make a card petal template and draw round it on the paper backing. You need one petal in each colour.

4 Cut out the shapes and peel off the backing.

5 Arrange the pieces on the bird shape and iron them on.

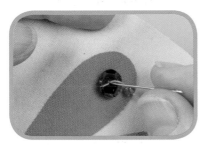

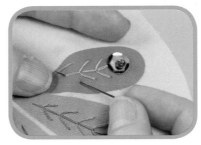

6 Sew a sequin and a bead on to the rounded edge of each petal shape as shown on page 17.

7 Choose a contrasting thread for each petal. Start at the sequin end and do closed fly stitch down each petal as shown on page 16.

8 Place the bird pieces right sides together and pin them. Use sewing thread to tack round the edge with large running stitches. Start 2cm (¾in) from the tail end, go round the bird and leave a 5cm (2in) gap on the bird's back. Fasten off and snip the end.

9 Thread up the machine and bobbin with cream thread. Set the gauge for a 1cm (⅜in) seam. Start 2cm (¾in) below the tail and sew to the tail corner. If you have a back stitch on your machine, do one here. With the needle down, lift up the foot.

10 Turn the fabric through 180°, put the foot down and go back over the sewing you have just done to begin sewing round the shape. Sew very slowly round the edge of the head, one stitch at a time. Keep to the 1cm (⅜in) gauge all the time.

11 Sew to the end of your tacking stitches, leaving the 5cm (2in) gap as before. Lift the foot with the needle up and slide the fabric out. Snip off the loose ends. Take out the pins, then cut and gently pull out the tacking stitches.

12 To keep the shape of the bird later, snip into the corners as shown, but do not snip right up to the stitching.

13 Trim round the edges and cut across the tail as shown. Do not trim across the gap.

14 Trim diagonally across the flaps that are left across the gap. Do this at each end of the gap.

15 Fold back the flaps and press them with your fingers to make a sharp fold.

16 Thread a needle with sewing thread and sew each flap to its side of the bird, to tidy the flaps.

17 Turn the bird right sides out. Use blunt-ended, closed scissors to push out the beak shape and the tail.

18 Stuff the bird with the kapok filling. Start with the head and beak and finish with the tail, pushing in small lumps at a time. Do not overstuff the bird or you will stretch the seams.

19 Use cream sewing thread to sew up the gap using ladder stitch as shown on page 17. Take out the tacking stitches.

TOP TIP!

Push very gently when pushing out the shapes, or your scissors will go through the fabric.

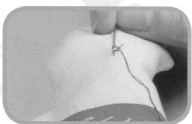

20 Make a few stitches where you want the bird's eye to be.

21 Sew on a sequin and a bead as shown on page 17. To finish, push the needle down through the sequin and up through the top of the head seam as shown. Snip off the thread close to the seam.

22 Place the ribbon as shown with both ends on the front of the bird. Sew through both ends and through both sides of the bird. Make four stitches and fasten off at the back. Use the same thread to sew on a button, as shown on page 17.

What next?

Try different shapes to decorate your bird, or use the hand appliqué method shown in the Perfect Picture project (pages 26–29). You may want to try making other simple shapes to decorate and stuff.

33

Throw Pillow

Decorate your bed with variations on this throw pillow design. They can either all have similar colours or be wildly different! Once you have mastered the machine appliqué technique, you could try inventing your own simple designs for throw pillow.

The patterns for the Throw Cushion, shown full size.

Patterns

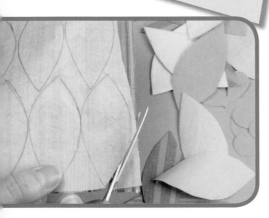

Photocopy the patterns and cut them out. Draw round them on card and cut out card templates. Apply fusible web to your four fabrics (see page 14). Draw round the leaf templates six times on each of the four fabrics. Make three daisies from one fabric, and three circles from a contrasting fabric.

2 Peel the backing off all the shapes.

3 Lay out the throw pillow front fabric and arrange the pieces as shown, with the fusible web side down. Allow at least 3cm (1¼in) between the shapes and the edge of the fabric.

4 Iron the shapes on to the throw pillow front fabric.

5 Put contrasting thread in the sewing machine's bobbin. Sew carefully round the circles 3mm (⅛in) from the edge. To decorate the flowers, begin near the end of a petal and sew to the centre. Sew to near the end of the next petal, then leave the needle in, lift the foot and turn the fabric round. Sew back to the centre and move on to the next petal.

6 Turn up the long edge of one of the back fabric pieces 1cm (3/8in) and iron the fold.

! STAY SAFE
Always have an adult with you when you are ironing.

! STAY SAFE
Always ask an adult to help you set up the sewing machine.

7 Fold the ironed edge over again and iron it again. Repeat steps 6 and 7 for the other back fabric piece.

8 Thread the sewing machine with matching sewing thread and sew just within the inner fold as shown. Repeat for the other back piece.

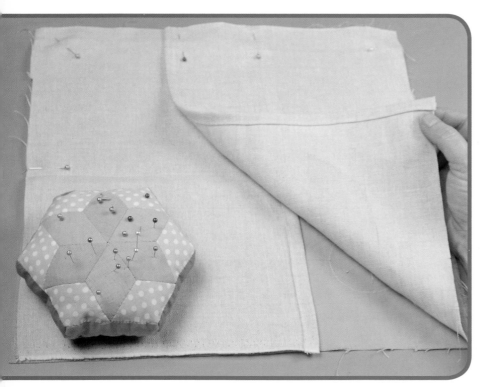

9 Pin the two back pieces to the wrong side of the front piece as shown.

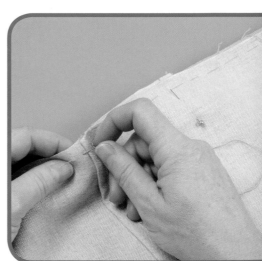

10 Tack the back pieces in place with long running stitches.

11 Set the sewing machine's gauge for a 1cm (⅛in) seam. Sew all the way round the edge of the throw cushion cover.

12 Remove the pins and the tacking. Snip across the corners, but do not cut as far as the stitching.

13 Turn the throw pillow cover right sides out. Push out the corners using blunt-ended, closed scissors. Now you can put in your cushion pad (pillow form).

The finished Throw Pillow.

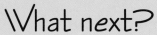

What next?

Using the same templates, you can create many different designs. Try using only the flower motif on a really bright background for a flower power throw pillow!

Pretty Pocket

This desirable little pocket hangs from your belt and is a great way to keep your phone or wallet near you at all times. Hand appliqué and machine sewing are both used to make it. It is an old idea brought up to date, as pockets always used to be separate pieces of clothing attached to a belt.

You will need

Card, pencil and scissors

Main fabric and lining fabric, 21 x 28cm (8¼ x 11in) each

Five plain fabric scraps and one patterned

Sewing threads to match all fabrics

White embroidery thread

Needle and pins

Iron

Sewing machine

Press stud (snap)

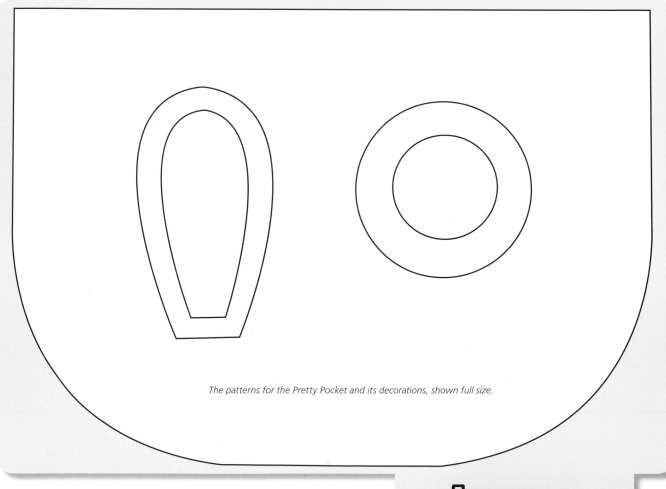

The patterns for the Pretty Pocket and its decorations, shown full size.

Patterns

1 Photocopy the pattern for the Pretty Pocket and cut out the shape. Draw round the shape twice on your main fabric and twice on your lining fabric and cut out the pieces. Also cut out two 16 x 4cm (6¼ x 1½in) pieces from the main fabric and two from the lining fabric, to make the belt hooks.

2 Cut out the larger petal shape from the photocopy and draw round it on card to make a template. Draw round it on five different scraps of fabric.

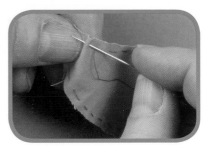

3 Thread a needle with sewing thread and sew in running stitch 3mm (⅛in) from the edge of a fabric petal. Do not trim the end of the thread.

4 Make a card template from the smaller petal shape and place it inside the fabric petal. Pull the tail of the thread to gather the edges.

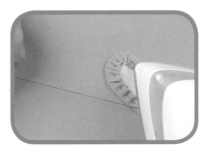

5 Iron the petal flat, secure and trim the end of the thread, then take out the small template.

STAY SAFE
Always have an adult with you when you are ironing.

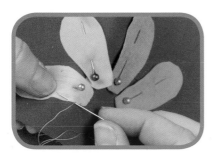

6 Make all the petals in the same way, then arrange them on the pocket shape and pin them in place. Sew each petal on using slip stitch (see page 15) in a matching sewing thread.

7 Use the larger circle pattern to cut out a circle from patterned fabric, then gather the edges around a card template made from the smaller circle pattern. Take out the template. Use slip stitch to sew on the circle in the centre of the petal design.

8 Use running stitch in white embroidery thread to sew round all the shapes.

9 To make a belt loop, place a main fabric piece and a lining piece right sides together. Set the sewing machine's gauge for a 1cm (⅜in) seam allowance. Thread it with thread to match the main fabric. Start to sew near the middle of a long side. Do a back stitch, then change to straight stitch. Sew for a few centimetres (1in), then turn and go back in the other direction. When you come to a corner, lift the foot with the needle in, turn the piece, lower the foot and continue. Sew right round the shape but leave a 6cm (2⅜in) gap in the long side where you started.

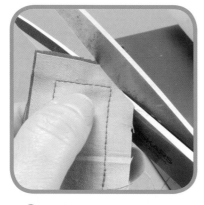

10 Snip off the corners and trim the edges so that the belt hook will be neater when it is turned right sides out. Make sure you do not cut up to the stitching.

11 Turn the belt hook right sides out and use closed, blunt scissors to push out the corners. Iron the belt hook flat.

12 Sew up the gap using ladder stitch (see page 17). Repeat steps 9–12 to make the second belt hook.

13 Place the embroidered bag front piece and a lining piece right sides together. Keeping to the 1cm (⅜in) seam allowance, sew across the top flat edge.

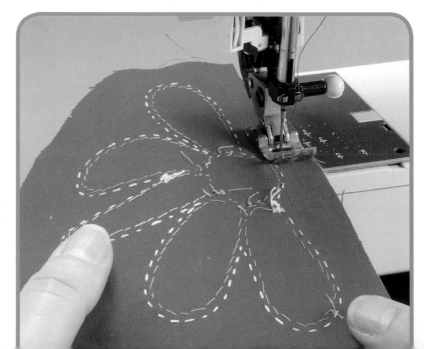

14 Repeat step 13 to sew together the plain back piece and the other lining piece.

15 Open the seams of the front and back pieces and iron them flat as shown.

16 Place the front and back pieces right sides together and line up the seams as shown.

18 Snip into all four curved edges, making sure you do not cut right up to the machine stitching.

17 Pin the front and back pieces together. Sew round the piece with a 1cm (⅜in) seam allowance, leaving a 6cm (2⅜in) opening in the rounded part of the lining.

19 Turn the pocket right sides out and push out the seams using closed, blunt scissors.

20 Sew up the gap using ladder stitch (see page 17) and sewing thread to match the lining.

21 Push the lining inside the pocket and iron the pocket.

22 Fold the belt hooks in half and place the ends just inside the back of the pocket as shown. Pin them in place.

23 Machine sew the belt hooks in place, sewing back and forth across the ends several times.

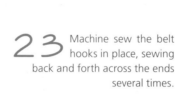

24 Thread a needle with doubled sewing thread and knot the end. Sew on half of a press stud (snap) in the centre of the pocket back. Hide the knot under the press stud. Sew through the lining only, not right through to the back of the pocket. Sew the other half on to the lining inside the front of the pocket.

The finished Pretty Pocket.

What next?

Make this pocket in different colours to match your favourite outfits, or use other motifs from the book to decorate it.

45

Felt Bag

This simple appliquéd bag can be decorated as much or as little as you like, and uses up the scraps of fabric you may have left over from other projects. It uses bias binding as a quick and simple edging. Try making it in colours to go with an outfit you love, or make a smaller version for a party. It would also make a lovely gift for a special friend.

You will need

Brown paper, pencil and scissors

Felt and lining fabric, ½m (19¾in) each

Fabric scraps and matching/contrasting sewing threads and embroidery threads

Fusible web and iron

Sewing machine

Needle, pins and buttons

Bias binding 1m (39½in)

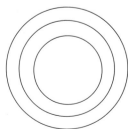

Patterns

The patterns for the Felt Bag and the designs on it, shown at half their actual size. You will need to enlarge them to 200 percent on a photocopier. The dotted line is the fold line at the bottom of the bag.

STAY SAFE

Always have an adult with you when you are ironing.

I Enlarge the bag pattern to its full size on a photocopier and cut out the shape. Draw round it to make a card template. Fold your felt in half and place the template so that the bottom line (dotted in the pattern) is on the fold. Draw round the template and cut out the bag shape. Do the same on your lining fabric.

2 Apply fusible web to your fabric scraps as shown on page 14. Make card templates for the circles, leaf and stalks. Draw round the templates and cut out shapes as follows: one large and one medium circle; four small circles; nine leaves; one large stalk and four smaller stalks. Trim the ends of two of the smaller stalks to make them shorter still. Peel off the backing.

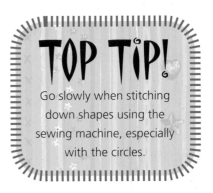

TOP TIP!

Go slowly when stitching down shapes using the sewing machine, especially with the circles.

3 Place all the shapes to create the design as shown and iron them on to the felt bag front.

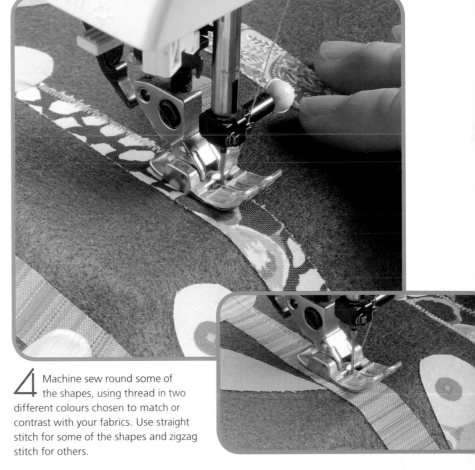

STAY SAFE

Always ask an adult to help you set up the sewing machine.

4 Machine sew round some of the shapes, using thread in two different colours chosen to match or contrast with your fabrics. Use straight stitch for some of the shapes and zigzag stitch for others.

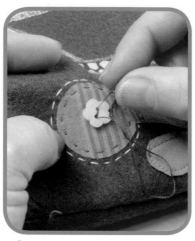

5 Hand sew round some of the shapes in running stitch using two strands of embroidery thread. Sew round the outsides of some of the flowers and leaves in the same way using either bright or white threads.

6 Sew a button in the centre of each flower (see page 17).

7 Turn the felt bag inside out and use a sewing machine and matching sewing thread to sew up the side seams, leaving a 1cm (⅜in) seam allowance.

8 Trim the corners, making sure you do not cut as far as the stitching.

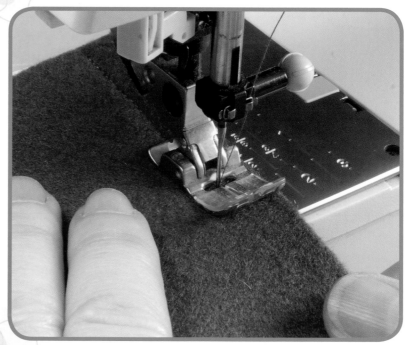

9 Sew across the top of the handle in the same way. Now repeat steps 7–9 to sew up the lining.

10 Put the lining in the bag, making sure you match up the seams of the lining with the seams of the bag.

11 Pin and tack the lining in place. Tack with large running stitches, 5mm (¼in) from the edge, round both the openings in the bag.

12 Take a length of bias binding and open up the fold on one side of it. Place it as shown just beyond the side seam of the felt bag. Fold over the end.

13 Pin the bias binding in place, following the curve of the bag's opening.

14 When you come back round to where you started, overlap the bias binding slightly, then trim the end. Tack the bias binding in place with long running stitches.

15 Machine sew the bias binding to the felt bag, leaving a 1cm (³⁄₈in) seam allowance. Sew slowly and carefully round the curves.

16 Fold the bias binding over the bag opening to hide the machine stitching. Slip stitch it in place (see page 15). Repeat steps 12–16 to complete the bag.

The finished bag.

Just by using different designs and colour ways you can adapt this simple bag to any style and taste. Try making a small one to take to a party!

EMBROIDERY

Claire Buckley

Embroidery is the wonderful craft in which fabrics are decorated with stitches, beads, sequins and other fabrics. This book will show you everything you need to start to embroider.

People have been creating fabulous effects on fabrics with embroidery for many thousands of years. The basic techniques have not altered, but fashions in embroidery – such as the way that we use colour, patterns and stitches – change over time, much like fashions in clothing.

Some of the Funky Facts tell you where the words that we use in embroidery come from, and this helps us to understand the history and origins of embroidery.

We can get lots of ideas for our embroidery by looking at embroideries from other countries and periods of time. Embroideries made in India are very inspirational in the way that they use colours, patterns and materials.

For each project you will find the basic instructions as well as tips on how to improve your embroidery and ideas for other things you could make. If you already know some of the basics, this section will help you to do even more exciting work with fabrics and threads.

FUNKY FACT!

Lots of the words that we use in embroidery come from France in the Middle Ages. This is possibly because when the Normans conquered England in 1066, the new French court brought their embroidery and language to England.

This bag from India uses mirrors (or sheesha), shells and metal, as well as stitches and beads to cover almost the entire surface of the fabric with decorations.

Glass beads are used to brighten the tassels on the corners of the bag. The bag is made from a square of fabric which is folded in like an envelope. The top flap is fastened by the cord being wrapped around the bag.

You should enjoy many happy hours creating wonderful embroideries for yourself, your family and your friends. There is nothing better than being able to say 'I made this'!

TOP TIP!

Try keeping a sketchbook in which you can collect all of your embroidery ideas by making drawings or sticking in exciting pictures, fabrics and other things you find in your everyday life.

Embroidery techniques

It is important to learn these basic techniques to get your embroidery off to a good start. When you have mastered the basics, you can go on to use more complicated techniques with different fabrics and stitches.

 Framing up

Many fabrics are too soft to stitch without being held tight in an embroidery frame. The most commonly used frame is the tambour ring. This is made of two wooden rings. The inner ring has to be covered with bias binding so that the fabric is not damaged when the outer ring is fixed over the inner ring, which holds the fabric tight.

1 Hold the bias binding firmly and start to wrap the inner hoop, taking care to overlap the previously laid section of binding as shown.

2 Continue wrapping the binding all the way around the hoop, making sure to keep the binding tight as you go.

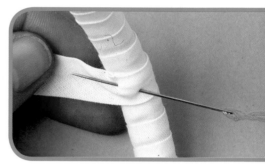

3 Thread your needle with stranded embroidery thread. Take the needle through the binding where it overlaps your starting point.

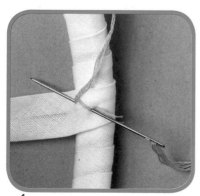

4 Take the needle through the binding again. This secures the binding with a 'back stitch'.

5 Place the covered ring flat on a table and lay the fabric right side up on top of the ring.

6 Place the outer ring of the frame on top of the fabric and inner ring. Tighten the screw fastener and pull the fabric until it is tight.

Preparing your thread and threading a needle

This is very easy to do. Lots of people use needle-threading gadgets, but you can simply hold the needle still in one hand and put the end of the thread into the eye of the needle.

1 Hold the label of the skein and pull the end of the thread until the thread reaches from your hand to your elbow, and cut it.

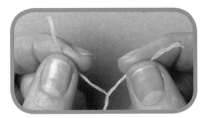

2 The thread is made of six strands and you need three strands to stitch. Divide the thread into two groups of three strands and pull them apart carefully.

3 Hold the needle still in one hand, flatten the end of the thread with your lips and push this through the eye of the needle.

 # Starting off

To hold the thread in place in the fabric, you need to sew a small 'back stitch' before you start to embroider.

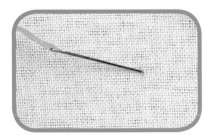

1 Push the needle through the fabric from the back. Pull the thread through, leaving a 1cm (⅜in) tail at the back of the fabric.

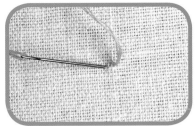

2 On the front of the fabric, push the needle back into the fabric close to where it came up. Pull the thread through tightly.

3 Now push the needle through to the front again where it first came up. Pull to tighten the stitch firmly. You are now ready to embroider!

 # Finishing off

1 On the back of the fabric, push the needle through one of the stitches near the end of your stitching.

2 Pull the thread gently until it forms a loop, then push the needle into the loop and pull the thread through.

3 Pull the thread tight to hold the stitches, then cut off the excess thread leaving a 1cm (⅜in) end.

Stitches

Running stitch

Running stitch is the most simple and useful stitch to learn.
It just goes up and down through the fabric.

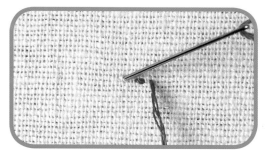

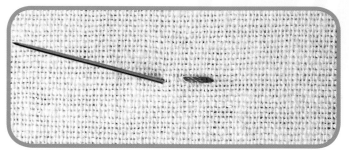

1 Start off by making a back stitch (see step 4 on page 54). Bring the needle up through the fabric to the right of the back stitch, and then back down to the left of the back stitch.

2 As you pull the thread tight, the back stitch will be covered neatly as shown. Working from right to left, bring the needle back up through the fabric and repeat.

TOP TIP!

If you are left-handed, work from left to right, rather than right to left.

A completed row of running stitch.

Running stitch is so simple, but it can be used to make all sorts of attractive designs.

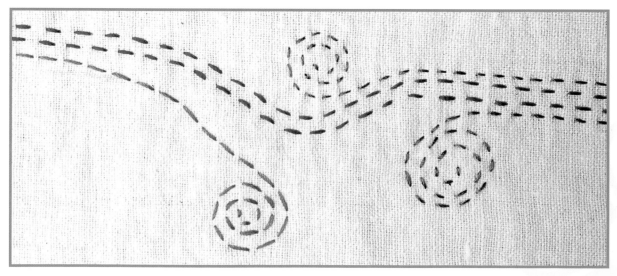

 # Chain stitch

Chain stitch is made up of interlocking loops or chains on the right side of the fabric.

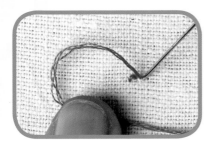

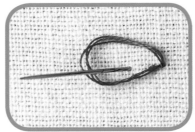

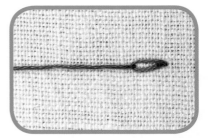

1 Make a back stitch, then bring the needle up through the fabric. Hold the loop of thread in place with your thumb, and pass the needle down next to the back stitch.

2 Bring the needle up through the loop.

3 Gently tighten the loop by pulling the thread tight.

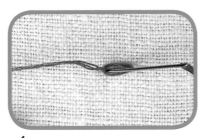

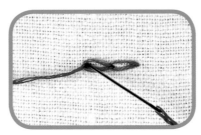

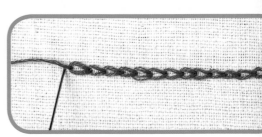

4 Start the next stitch by passing the needle down inside the loop of the last one.

5 Repeat steps 2–4 until the chain is as long as you need it.

6 Finish off your row with a small stitch to fix the thread.

A completed row of chain stitch.

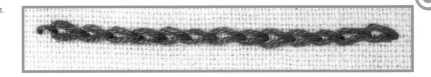

Chain stitch can be used to make attractive designs as well as basic lines.

☀ Fly stitch

Fly stitch is like a single chain stitch, but the loop is not closed or fixed at one point. This makes the stitch very useful because you can change the length of each part of the 'Y' shape. Try to overlap the stitches for a decorative effect, or stitch in rings to make stars.

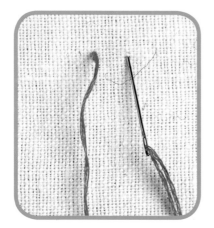

1 Bring the needle up through the fabric, then back down, creating an open loop, which lies towards you.

2 Bring the needle back up through the fabric, creating a 'V' shaped loop.

3 Bring the needle over the 'V' shape and down through the fabric, pulling the thread tight.

TOP TIP!

It is easiest to work fly stitch sideways from right to left.

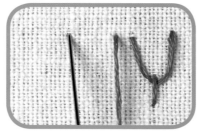

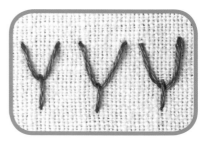

4 Start the next stitch to the left of the last one.

A completed row of fly stitch.

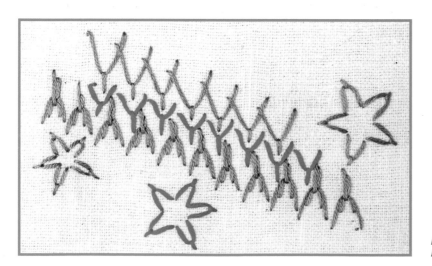

Fly stitch can be interlocked to create beautiful patterns.

Blanket stitch

This is called blanket stitch as it is used to neaten the edges of blankets. For a more decorative effect, try overlapping the stitches in different lengths and colours.

1 On the back of the fabric near the edge, make a back stitch to start off the thread. With the back of the fabric still facing you, put the needle back through to create a loop as shown.

2 Turn the fabric over, and take the needle through the loop.

3 Gently tug the thread to close the loop. This will anchor the end of the row of stitches.

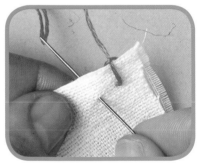

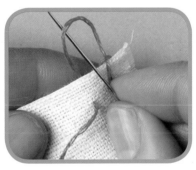

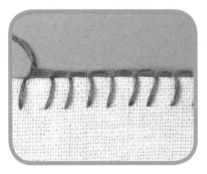

4 Pull the needle through the fabric to create a loop.

5 Put the needle back through the loop at the edge of the fabric.

A completed row of blanket stitch.

TOP TIP!
This stitch is brilliant to add a decorative edge to pieces of fabric.

Blanket stitch looks good when overlapped in different lengths and colours.

Cross stitch

Cross stitch can be used singly, in lines, or in groups to make your design. Vary the size and shape of your cross stitches. For example, imagine a four-sided shape and fit the stitch across the shape from corner to corner.

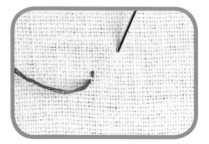

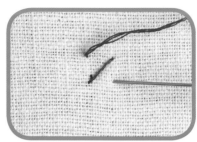

I Start the thread off with a back stitch, then bring the needle up at the bottom left point and push the needle in at the top right point.

2 Take the thread across the back and come up at the top left point, go across the front and down at the bottom right.

3 Pull the thread until an 'x' is made. This is the first stitch. Push the needle up again ready for the next stitch.

A completed row of cross stitch.

Couching

Couching is used when you want to use a thread that is too thick to go easily through your fabric, so it is laid on top and held in place by small stitches – often in a different colour. You should start by taking the end of the couching thread through to the back of the fabric to make it neat and fix it in place.

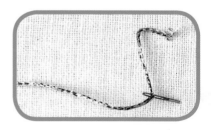

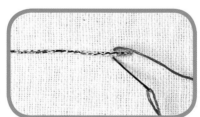

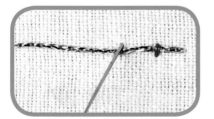

I Thread a tapestry needle with the thick couching thread. From the front of the fabric push the needle into the fabric where you want to start couching. Remove the tapestry needle.

2 Use a thin thread with an embroidery needle to make small stitches over the couching thread.

3 Continue stitching along the length of the couching thread. At the end re-thread the couching thread on the tapestry needle and push it to the back of the work to neaten the threads, fasten with the thin thread.

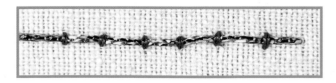

A completely couched thread.

French knots

French knots can be used to add texture and detail to your embroidery.

1 Start by making a back stitch, then bring the needle up and wrap the thread around the needle.

2 Continue wrapping the thread around the needle to form a spiral. The more times you wrap the thread around, the bigger the final knot.

3 Push the needle back through the fabric near where you came up and pull the thread through to create the knot.

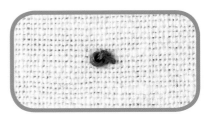

A completed French knot.

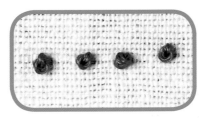

A row of French knots.

FUNKY FACT!

In France a 'French knot' is called *le point de noeud*. This means 'the spot where the knot is'.

TOP TIP!

Do not worry if the knots do not all come out looking tight. The loose texture can look as good as tight knots on your work.

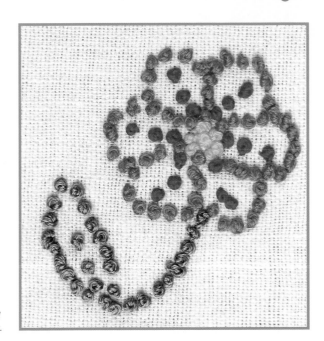

A flower made up of different-coloured French knots.

Embellishments

This is where the fun really starts with your embroidery. You can go mad adding all sorts of decorations (called embellishments) to make your embroidery really personal. Look out for unusual sequins, beads and buttons in shops.

☼ Sequins

I Thread your needle and bring it up through the fabric and through the hole in the centre of the sequin.

2 Place the sequin where you want it and take the needle through the fabric at the top of the sequin.

3 Fix the sequin by pulling the thread tight. Finish off or continue sewing sequins on your design.

Beads

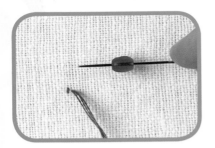  

1 Make a back stitch, then bring your threaded needle up through the fabric and put the bead on to it.

2 Push the needle back through the fabric close to where you came up, and pull the thread tight.

3 This will fix the bead in place. Carry on adding beads this way to make your design.

 ## Sequin and bead combination

It is fun to hold sequins in place with a bead. Try to experiment with different sizes and colours of beads and sequins.

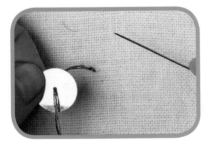 

1 Place the sequin where you want it to sit, and bring your threaded needle up through the centre of the sequin.

2 Pick up the bead on to the needle. You might like to use more than one bead.

There are hundreds of different designs of beads and sequins you can use.

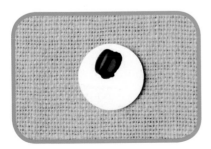

3 Push the needle back through the centre of the sequin and pull the thread gently to tighten.

Buttons

Buttons are very easy to sew on to fabric, and make great simple decorations for embroidered pieces. To attach the buttons very firmly, simply sew them on with two or three stitches rather than one.

Two-hole buttons

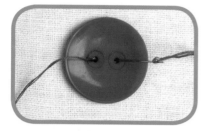

1 Thread the needle as usual, then place the button and come up through one of the holes. Put the needle in the second hole.

2 Take the needle down through the second hole, pull the thread to hold the button in place and fasten off as usual.

Four-hole buttons

To sew four-hole buttons on, it is fun to do a cross stitch as it makes it look more interesting.

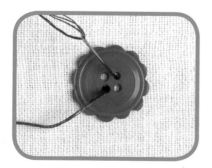

1 Place the button, and bring your threaded needle up through the bottom left hole and down through the top right hole.

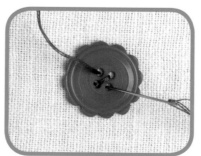

2 Bring the needle up through the top left hole and down through the bottom right hole. Fasten off at the back as usual.

The button sewn on with a cross stitch.

Mock sheesha

Sheesha is the Hindi word for 'mirror' and comes from the Persian for 'fragment'. It can also be spelt *shisha*. Sheesha are usually small round mirrors, but they can also be square, as seen on the bag on page 52. When the sun shines on the mirror, the bright reflection gives the illusion that the embroidery has expensive jewels on it.

Mock sheesha are made of two parts, a plastic ring covered with coloured stitches and a round silver disc like a sequin without a hole.

1 Anchor the ring with a small stitch, then start to sew the ring in place with neat running stitches through the coloured stitches of the ring.

2 When you are halfway round, slide the silver disc under the ring.

3 Carry on stitching until you have gone the whole way round, then knot the thread at the back of the fabric to secure it.

Silver mock sheesha and craft jewels. The jewels are sewn on like sequins.

Peacock Picture

You will need

HB pencil

White cotton lawn, 30cm (12in) square

Turquoise cotton, 30cm (12in) square

Turquoise/rust organza, 30cm (12in) square

20cm (8in) tambour ring

Embroidery needle

Stranded embroidery threads in blue, green and purple

Five craft jewels

Thick gold thread

Tapestry needle

Sequins

Pins

Two 10cm (4in) lengths of narrow ribbon

Embroidered pictures are a great way to decorate your room and show off your embroidery skills. This lovely picture is inspired by designs from India. It uses some of the basic techniques with stitches, sequins and craft jewels and has loops so that you can hang it on your wall.

TOP TIP!

The white cotton lawn is placed behind the top fabrics to support and add strength to your embroidery, as the stitches and jewels can get quite heavy.

The pattern for the Peacock Picture, reproduced at actual size.

66

1 Trace the pattern directly on to the turquoise cotton lawn fabric, using the HB pencil.

2 Layer the three fabrics with the white cotton lawn at the back, turquoise cotton in the middle and the organza on the top. Hold them together with a pin.

3 Put the fabrics into the tambour ring, ensuring that the design is in the centre. Remember to pull the fabrics tight!

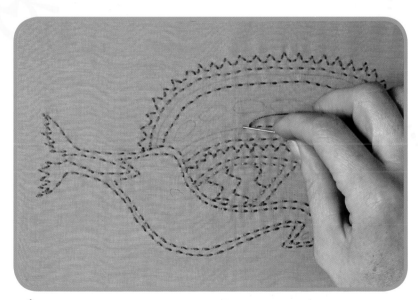

4 Thread your needle with the blue embroidery thread and outline the design with running stitch. Keep the stitches quite small and regular to ensure that the peacock looks neat. Once the blue outline is completed, use the green and purple threads to add running stitch details as shown.

5 The running stitch completed.

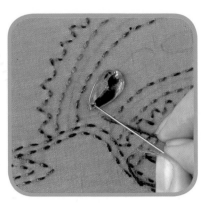

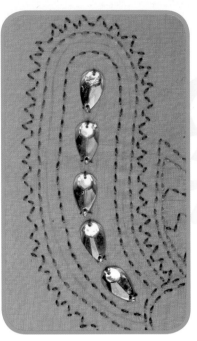

6 Attach the first craft jewel on to the tail through the bottom hole, following the instructions for attaching sequins on page 62. Do not fasten off the thread yet.

7 Secure the jewel by coming up through the fabric and back down through the hole at the bottom of the craft jewel. Tie off the end of the thread at the back of the fabric.

8 Take the thread through the top of the craft jewel to finish, then sew on the other jewels, as shown, until the tail is complete.

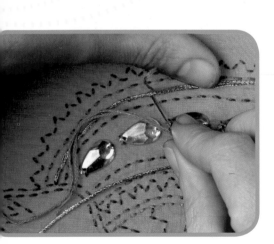

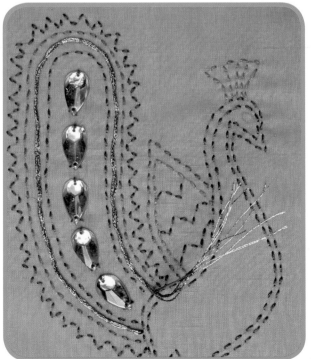

9 Place the gold thread on the tapestry needle, bring it up through the tail and lay it down, following the line. Thread the embroidery needle with purple thread and couch the gold thread all the way along, following the instructions on page 60.

10 Once you have finished couching, re-thread the gold thread on the tapestry needle and take it through the fabric. Remove the needle and tie off the gold thread at the back.

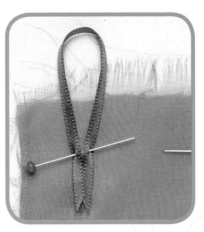

11 Sew the sequins on to the peacock's body, eye and the crown of the head, as shown above, following the instructions on page 62.

12 Remove the embroidery from the tambour ring. Secure the edges with pins. This holds the three layers of fabric in place so that you can sew the edges.

13 At each of the top corners of the fabric, pin a loop of ribbon.

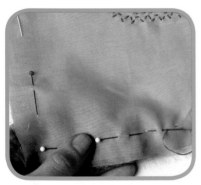

14 Start to stitch the edge using running stitch, removing the pins as you get to them.

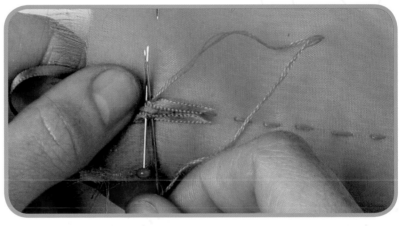

15 Fix the ribbons in place with a small back stitch as you get to them.

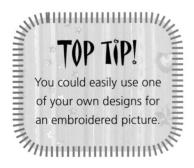

TOP TiP!

You could easily use one of your own designs for an embroidered picture.

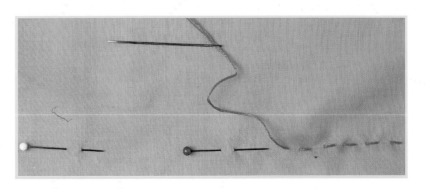

16 Continue stitching the edges, removing the pins as you go.

The finished Peacock Picture.

What next?

The ideas here show how the design can easily be changed.

Try using different sequins and jewels on the body, tail and edges.

You could also use a different design of a peacock to make a pair of wall hangings, or use couching on the edges as well as in the design.

Make a cushion from the embroidery by using a fabric that looks good with the embroidered picture.

Funky Book Cover

You will need

- White cotton calico
- Orange netting
- Blue coloured cotton for the lining
- Notebook
- Chocolate wrappers
- Large scissors
- Glue stick
- Embroidery needle
- Stranded embroidery threads in blue, red and yellow
- Elephant and circle sequins
- Blue ribbon and star button for the bookmark

If you like chocolates then you will love collecting the wrappers for this project. The shiny foils and plastic wrappers are perfect to make this beautiful, colourful book cover. This project is quick to make and would be perfect as a present for your family or friends.

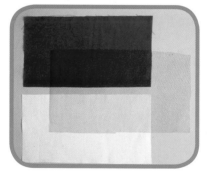

1 Cut the white cotton calico, netting and coloured cotton to the same size as your opened notebook plus a 1cm (⅜in) border at the top and bottom, and a 4cm (1½in) border on each side.

2 Cut the wrappers into small squares. Make sure that the squares are all the same size.

TOP TIP!

You could use photographs or postage stamps in place of the wrappers to make the project more personal.

3 Lay out the wrappers into your design and attach them to the white cotton calico using the glue stick.

TOP TIP!

The colour of the netting will change the look of the wrappers. Experiment with different coloured netting to get the effect that you want for your cover.

4 Continue sticking the wrappers on to the white cotton calico.

5 Lay the net over the wrappers and fabric and pin it on. The net protects the wrappers from being knocked off or damaged.

6 Work chain stitch diagonally across the cover in a stepped shape round the squares as shown. Use three different coloured threads. This will secure the netting to the fabric.

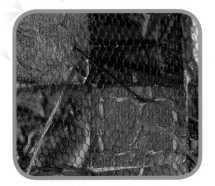

7 Work running stitch within some of the squares for decoration and extra strength. Again, vary the colours of the threads you use.

8 Sew on the sequins. Round and elephant-shaped sequins have been used here, but you could use any sort of sequin that you want.

You should now have a cover that looks like this.

9 Turn the book cover over and pin the blue cotton lining on to it.

10 Trim the excess fabric off the sides of the book cover with a pair of large scissors.

11 Edge both of the short ends with blanket stitch.

Detail of the stitching and decorations.

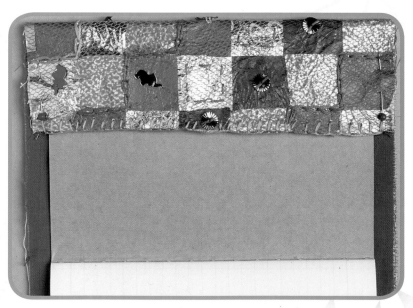

12 Put the notebook inside the cover and fold the excess fabric over the book's covers; making sure you have equal amounts of the fabric on both sides.

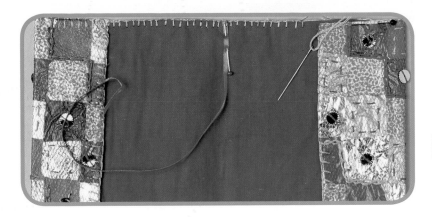

13 Remove the notebook and use blanket stitch to secure the long edges as shown. Stitch a length of ribbon into the centre of the top edge to make the bookmark.

14 Put the notebook into the cover and tie a small star button to the ribbon.

The finished Funky Book Cover.

What next?

Add buttons and cut wrappers into the shape of your initials to personalise your book cover (left).

A large sketchbook is useful to collect all of your design ideas, so make a beautiful cover (centre). This one has chocolate coin wrappers with sequins (in lots of different shapes and sizes); beads and fly stitch in circles; and an extra large button on the bookmark.

Use the wrappers and cross stitch to make the spine of the book stand out. Attach a red foil heart to make a perfect present (right).

Magic Bag

You will need

- Pink striped cotton rectangle, 27 x 14cm (10½ x 5½in)
- Purple cotton lawn rectangle, 40 x 16cm (15¾ x 6in)
- Pins and small safety pin
- Ruler and scissors
- Stranded embroidery threads in purple and pink
- Embroidery needle
- Tapestry needle
- A selection of beads, sequins and craft jewels
- Purple and pink narrow ribbons, each 50cm (19¾in)
- Two 40cm (15¾in) lengths of silver metallic thread
- Two small squares of pink fabric

This magic bag will fool everyone until they know the secret of how to open it using the handles. You pull one set to close the bag and the other set to open it. You can also use your imagination and the other techniques in the book to add extra decoration to the bag and the handles.

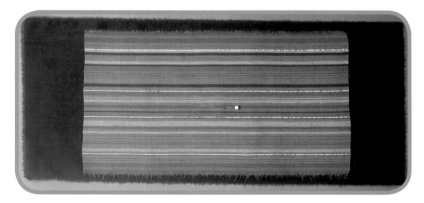

Place the smaller rectangle in the middle of the larger rectangle and use a pin to hold them together.

TOP TiP!

To get the lovely frayed edges for the bag, tear the fabric to the correct size. Do this by measuring the fabric, making a small cut in the edge and then tearing the fabric.

2 Thread the needle with purple embroidery thread, and sew the two rectangles together using cross stitches on the long sides of the smaller rectangle as shown.

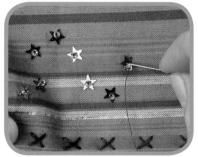

3 Add sequins with beads to build your design.

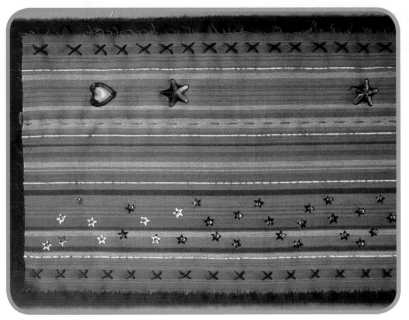

5 To make the channel for the ribbon handles, fold the short sides of the larger rectangle over the ends of the smaller rectangle. Pin in place.

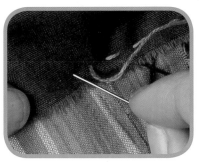

4 Add more embroidery stitches to decorate the pink fabric and help secure it to the purple fabric. I have used pink running stitches that follow the stripes on the fabric. Add the craft jewels to the bag as shown, following the instructions for sewing on sequins on page 62.

6 Sew the ribbon channel in place with small running stitches. Once this is done, repeat at the other end of the bag.

7 Fold the bag in half, by bringing the ribbon channels together, and pin in place. Use small running stitches to sew up the side but make sure that you keep the ribbon channels open at the top.

8 Start and finish this stitching carefully so that it is strong enough to hold the bag together. Repeat on the other side.

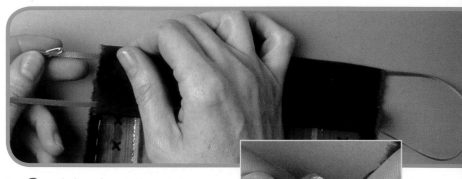

9 To add the ribbon handles, fix a safety pin to the purple ribbon. Thread the safety pin all the way through the ribbon channel.

10 Push the safety pin through the other ribbon channel so that is goes right round the bag. Remove the safety pin and tie the ends of the ribbon in a knot (see inset).

TOP TIP!
Do not pull the safety pin too hard, as you could pull the ribbon right through the channels. It is a good idea to secure the end of the ribbon to the opening of the channel with a pin before you start threading the safety pin through the channel.

11 Pass the pink ribbon through the channels from the other side of the bag and tie off as before.

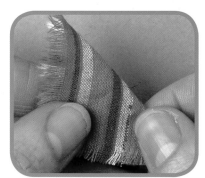

12 Thread the tapestry needle with one length of the thick silver thread. Take the threaded needle through the lower edge of the ribbon channel as shown.

13 Pull the thread halfway through, remove the needle and tie the ends with a knot. Repeat with the other length of silver thread on the other side of the bag.

14 Take one of the small squares of fabric and fold it in half diagonally.

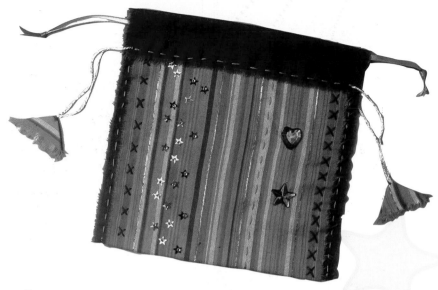

15 Fold the fabric in half diagonally again to form a smaller triangle. Wrap this around the knot on the silver thread, and attach the fabric to the knot with a small stitch.

16 Attach another square of fabric on the other side.

17 You can close the Magic Bag by pulling the coloured ribbons, and open it using the silver threads.

The finished Magic Bag is perfect for keeping treasures inside.

What next?

Use contrasting fabrics and couching to decorate the bag. Add decorations to all the handles.

Go mad with shiny fabrics and large sequins to make a gorgeous gift bag.

Make a large backpack with recycled denim. Decorate with frayed fabrics and buttons, then make the straps from strong cord.

FUNKY FACT!

This project was inspired by this small bag with two sets of drawstrings. The curved shape makes a circle when the handles are pulled shut.

Heart Purse

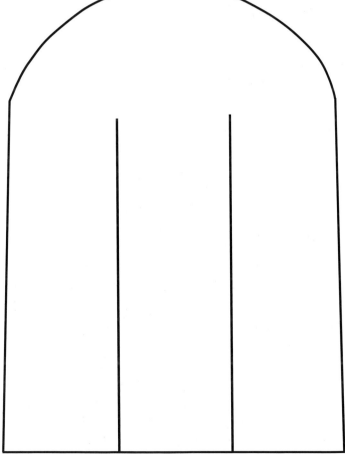

This heart-shaped purse is made from two pieces of folded felt woven together. The <u>weaving</u> is quick to do but the way that you decorate the purse is up to you. The decoration also holds the weaving together, stopping the fabrics from slipping apart. I have used mock sheesha, French knots and a heart button to fasten the purse.

The pattern for the Heart Purse, shown at actual size.

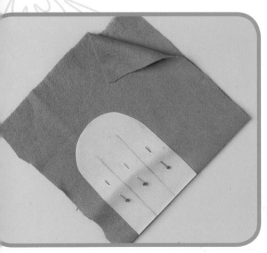

Use the pencil to trace the pattern on to a sheet of tracing paper and cut it out. Fold the felt. Place the straight edge of the pattern on the fold and pin it in place.

Place this end on the fold in the felt.

84

2 Use the scissors to cut around the pattern and along the lines as shown.

3 Repeat this process with the purple felt. The folded felt makes loops that are woven together to form the heart purse.

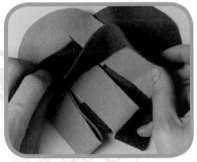

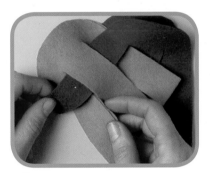

4 Begin to weave the purple felt into the blue felt as follows: Put the first blue loop through the first purple loop.

5 Put this purple loop through the second blue loop.

6 Put the third blue loop through the purple loop.

7 Now weave the second purple loop by putting it through the first blue loop.

85

8 Put the second blue loop through the second purple loop.

9 Put the second purple loop through the third blue loop.

10 Now weave the final purple loop by putting the first blue loop through it.

11 Put the third purple loop through the second blue loop.

12 Finally, the third blue loop goes through the third purple loop. Pull the purse into shape. You can open the purse because of the way the two sides of the loops fit together.

TOP TIP!

Hold the purse open with your fingers while embroidering the decorations so that the two sides are not sewn together.

13 Sew the mock sheesha on to the purple squares of the weaving, following the instructions on page 65.

14 Stitch French knots into the blue squares, following instructions on page 61.

15 Sew on the button at the top of the front of the purse.

16 Add French knots and mock sheesha on to the back of the purse as shown.

17 Fold the ribbon in half. Sew it on with a small back stitch on the inside of the back of the purse. Make sure that you can fasten the purse by placing the ribbon over the button.

The finished Heart Purse.

What next?

Make a lovely shoulder bag by enlarging the pattern on a photocopier. For each side cut two pieces of each fabric and blanket stitch all of the edges before weaving. I have used denim and satin for the shoulder bag opposite. Decorate with jewels and embroidery stitches. Add buttons and ribbon loops to fasten and a long ribbon as a strap.

Weave red fabric together and embroider with cream running stitches along the edges.

Weave two pieces of denim together, with the pale side of one piece on the outside. Decorate with wavy lines of chain stitch.

Use two colours of felt and decorate with lots of buttons, then add cross stitches at each corner of the squares.

Lucky Charms

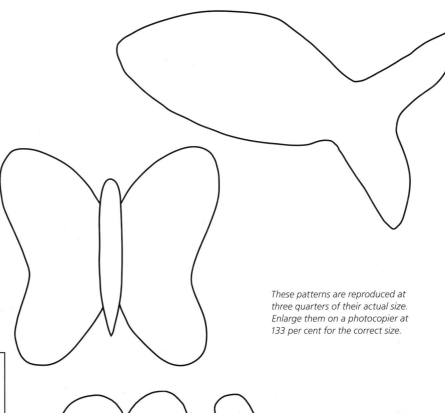

These embroidered felt charms
are quick and easy to make. They
use small amounts of felt so they do not cost too
much. You can experiment with lots of ideas of your own
and give them as presents to all of your friends and family.

You will need

- Tracing paper
- HB pencil
- Grey felt
- Pins
- Large scissors
- Embroidery needle
- Pink and yellow stranded embroidery threads
- A selection of sequins and beads
- Polyester wadding (batting)
- Silver metallic thread

These patterns are reproduced at three quarters of their actual size. Enlarge them on a photocopier at 133 per cent for the correct size.

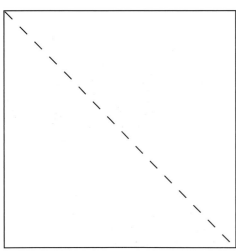

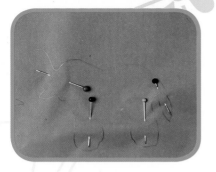

1 Trace the elephant pattern, and pin the tracing to the felt.

2 Cut out the elephant, and remove the pins.

3 Turn the elephant over and pin the tracing on to the felt again. Cut out the second elephant shape.

4 Decorate one side of the elephant with pink chain stitch lines. To make a more interesting end to the line, make a long stitch over the last chain loop as normal, but do not tie the thread off.

5 Take the thread back into the last loop of the chain, and make a second and third stitch to either side of the first stitch, as shown.

6 Use yellow stranded embroidery thread to mark the elephant's ear with a line of running stitch.

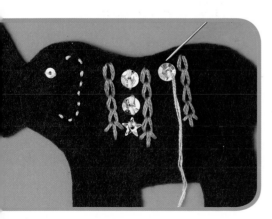

7 Sew sequins on to the elephant between the rows of chain stitch to build the design as shown. Sew on a small sequin as an eye.

8 Decorate the other side of the second elephant in the same way. Remember that it is important to get a pair of elephants facing each other so that the decorations remain on the outside when you sew the elephants together.

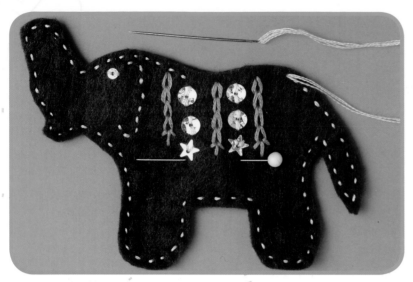

9 Put the two elephants together and pin. Sew with small running stitches near to the edge, but leave a small gap open at the top of the elephant.

10 Push a small amount of polyester wadding (batting) into the elephant to pad it out.

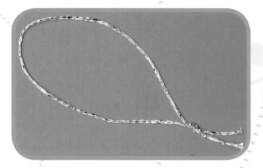

11 Make a loop by knotting the silver metallic thread as shown.

12 Place the knot into the gap at the top of the elephant and sew up the gap with running stitch.

The finished Lucky Charm.

What next?

Use the patterns on page 90 to make other lucky charms, and decorate them with buttons, beads, sequins and embroidery stitches. You could use a key ring fastening instead of the thread loop.

Heart: Use chain stitch and buttons.

Fish: This is decorated with spirals of running stitch and a heart-shaped sequin. It has a key ring fixed to it so you can use the charm to hold your keys.

Triangle: Start with a square of felt, decorate it and then fold it in half to make the triangle. The silver metal charms look good hanging off the shape.

Butterfly: Use fly stitch and sequins to show the markings of the butterfly.

Circle: Decorate with snowflake sequins and star jewels.

TOP TIP!

If you are using an asymmetrical shape, remember to turn the second side over so that you have two shapes that fit together.

PATCHWORK

Nancy Nicholson

From very early times people have made things to use up and reuse old clothes. Patchwork quilts were a way of recycling old clothes, as well as being a necessary source of warmth. Necessity makes for the best ideas! If you look at pictures of old patchwork quilts, you can see good examples of the fabrics used in the clothes of the time – patchwork has always been a great way to remember favourite garments. In the United States in the 19th century, groups of women would get together to finish their quilts, and these were called 'Quilting Bees'. The Shakers of America have provided us with wonderful inspiration which can be seen still today, using up scraps of their clothing.

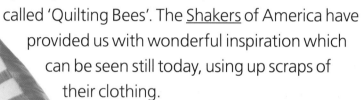

Today patchwork is still a great way to recycle. You can begin your collection of fabric straight away. Ask friends and family for old clothes or scraps of fabric they may have left over, or search in charity shops for interesting and colourful fabrics. It is fun building up your collection, and you should iron, fold and sort your fabric scraps to make designing easy.

I came to patchwork as a child, making dolls' clothes out of scraps of fabric given to me by my mother. I went on to make simple quilts, though it was collecting the materials as much as anything that I loved, and now I have bags and bags of scraps everywhere! I began with hand patchwork and loved cutting out the paper templates, gradually making enough to begin sewing them together. When my children were little, I made them many things, from toys and bibs to quilts and clothes. My oldest son loves to customise his own clothes and my youngest spends hours designing T-shirts and trainers. I hope you will love patchwork too!

Patchwork techniques

Machine stitching

You can use a sewing machine to sew the patchwork pieces together.

1 Line up your fabric carefully. Use the gauge to set a 1cm (⅜in) seam allowance and lower the machine's foot.

2 Set the machine to straight stitch. Press the foot pedal to sew.

3 When you have finished sewing, lift up the foot, slide out the sewn fabric and snip the threads.

Turning a corner

To turn a corner when machine sewing, stop at the corner with the needle in the fabric. Lift the foot, turn the piece you are sewing, put the foot down again and continue sewing.

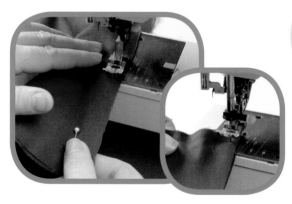

Using craft interfacing

This is used to stiffen the fabric in some projects.

Cut out the craft interfacing and position it sticky side down on your fabric. Press it with a hot iron to attach it to the fabric.

Ladder stitch

This is very useful for sewing up the gaps that you leave in some pieces if you need to turn them right sides out and stuff them. You should do ladder stitch in a matching thread.

1 To sew up a gap in a piece, come up through the machine stitching to hide the knot inside the piece.

2 Make a small stitch along the fold on one side of the gap.

3 Pull through and make another small stitch along the fold on the other side of the gap. Continue until the whole gap is sewn up.

4 To fasten off, go back under the machine stitching and up again. Repeat several times and trim.

The finished seam.

Oversewing

You can also close up a gap by oversewing as shown below.

Thread a needle and knot the end of the thread. Bring the needle up from the wrong side of the fabric. Push the needle through the edges of both the pieces of fabric you are joining. Pull it through, then push the needle through again further along in the same direction, and so on until you have sewn together the edges. Fasten off by making several stitches on top of each other, then snip the ends.

Pet's Blanket

Make an adorable miniature blanket for your cat or dog, to line their basket. Choose bright colours which they will enjoy!

You will need

Paper or plastic for templates

Ballpoint pen or pencil

Six different fabric scraps for the patchwork top

Cotton backing fabric, 42cm (16½in) square

Four pieces of binding fabric: two 6 x 45cm (2⅜ x 17¾in) and two 6 x 54cm, (2⅜ x 21¼in) or bias binding

Sewing machine

Iron

Machine thread to contrast with your patchwork pieces

Wadding, 51cm (20in) square

Needle, pins, tacking thread, thread to match the binding fabric and thick, bright embroidery thread

1 Make a 10cm (4in) square template from paper or plastic. Draw round it on six different fabrics and cut five squares from each fabric. I have cut out five pink, five yellow, five orange and five each in three different checked fabrics.

2 Lay the squares out in the pattern you have chosen for your quilt.

3 Pick up the squares one by one and stack them in a row on the right-hand side.

4 Thread up the sewing machine with contrasting thread (I have used red). Sew the top square from the first stack to the second square. Place the squares right sides together and sew along one side with a 1cm (³⁄₈in) seam allowance.

5 Sew the third square to the second square in the same way and continue through the whole stack to make one row. Then sew the second stack in the same way, and so on. Iron the seams open, then iron the front of each row.

6 Place two rows right sides together and match up the seams carefully. Machine sew along a long edge with a 1cm (³⁄₈in) seam allowance.

7 Continue in this way, sewing each row to the next row. When the quilt front is all sewn together, iron the seams open as before. Iron the front as well.

8 Layer the backing fabric, then the wadding, then the front piece. Line them up carefully.

9 Pin the three layers in place as shown. Place a pin in each corner and one in the middle, then one in the middle of each side.

10 Thread a needle with tacking thread. Starting in the middle of one side, tack across the middle to the other side. Repeat across the middle in the other direction. Then tack along each edge as shown.

11 Fold down the long edge of a binding piece 1cm (³⁄₈in) and iron it down. Repeat on the other side. Do this for all four binding pieces.

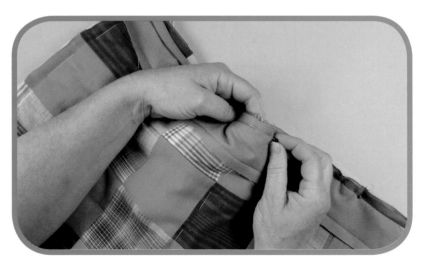

12 Place a long binding piece right sides together along a long edge of the quilt and pin along the fold.

13 Tack along the fold line. Thread up the machine with matching thread and sew with a 1cm (³⁄₈in) seam allowance. Repeat steps 12 and 13 for the other long edge.

14 Fold the binding over to the back of the quilt and pin it in place. Line it up carefully to cover the stitching.

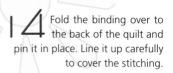

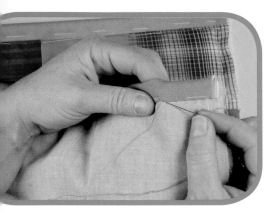

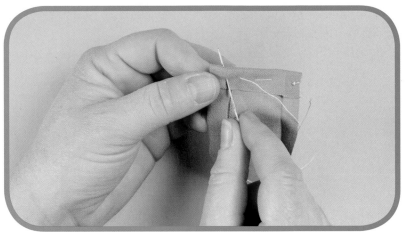

15 Tack the binding in place and remove the pins. Oversew with matching thread. Repeat steps 14 and 15 to complete both long edges.

16 Fold down the end of a shorter binding piece and tack it in place with one side folded down and one side open as shown.

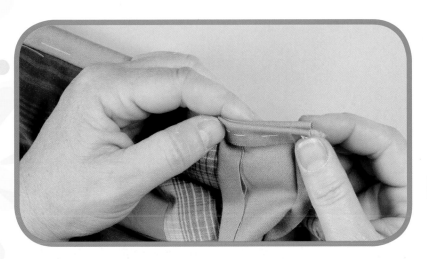

17 Line up the folded end with the end of a long bound edge of the quilt as shown. Pin the binding down the short edge along the fold as before.

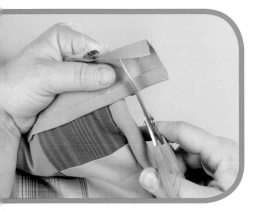

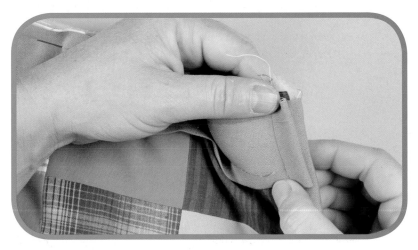

18 At the other end, cut off any excess binding, leaving a 1cm (³⁄₈in) overhang.

19 Fold back the end as in step 17. Tack the binding on as for the long sides.

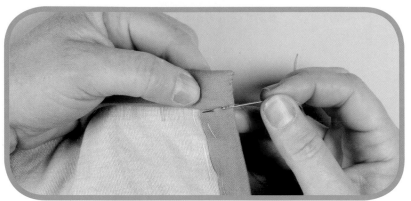

20 Machine sew along the short edge as before. Repeat steps 16 to 20 for the other short edge.

21 Turn over the binding to the back of the quilt, then tack into position. Oversew along the corner, then turn the quilt and oversew along the short edge as before. Take the tacking stitches out and trim all the ends of thread.

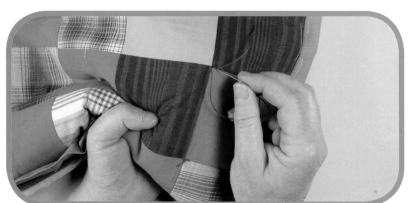

22 Thread a needle with bright, thick embroidery thread. Go in from the front of the quilt into a point between squares. Leave a 6cm (2³⁄₈in) tail. Come up 5mm (¼in) away and go down where you first came up.

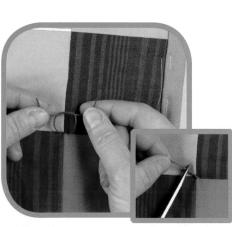

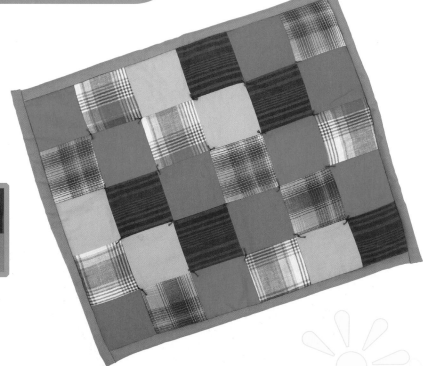

23 Come up again, trim the thread to a 6cm (2³⁄₈in) tail and knot the two tails. Knot two more times and trim the ends. Make a similar knot at all the points between squares.

What next?

Try making a bigger blanket as a cover for your bed. You could even put some simple appliqué shapes on the squares before you sew them together.

Pin Cushion

This is such a quick and easy project to make and you can use your pin cushion for all your other patchwork projects. Once you have made one pin cushion, you will want to try other combinations of fabric and shapes.

The patterns for the Pin Cushion, shown three-quarters of actual size. You will need to enlarge them to 133% on a photocopier.

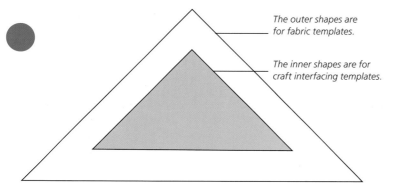

The outer shapes are for fabric templates.

The inner shapes are for craft interfacing templates.

TOP TIP!

As long as you cut out your pin cushion pieces accurately, they should fit together beautifully.

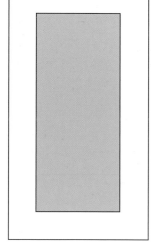

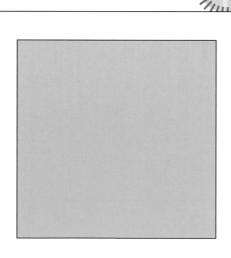

1 Photocopy the patterns, cut them out and draw round them on card to make templates. Draw round the templates on fabric to make two large patterned triangles, two plain triangles, four rectangles and one square.

2 Make smaller card templates from the inner shapes of the patterns. Draw round them on craft interfacing and cut out four rectangles, four triangles and a square.

3 Place the craft interfacing shapes face down on the back of the fabric shapes and iron them down, leaving an even border around them.

4 Thread a needle with a single thread and knot the end. Fold down the edge of a shape over the craft interfacing and tack it in place. When you get to the next side, fold it down and do a stitch over the overlap to hold the corner down. Tack round all the pieces in this way.

5 Lay a patterned and a plain triangle side by side as shown, then place them right sides together. Thread a needle with a matching thread and knot the end. Come up through both triangles and oversew along the edge (see page 97).

6 At the other end, sew over the same spot three or four times to secure the stitching, then trim the thread.

7 Sew together the other two triangles in the same way, then sew the two pairs together. Match up the seams carefully as shown and start sewing in the middle.

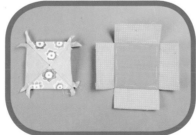

8 Sew the rectangles to the square in the same way so that you have a flattened box shape and a lid shape as shown.

9 Stitch up the short sides of two of the rectangles with the craft interfacing on the outside (or 'wrong sides out'). You will begin to see a three-dimensional box shape.

10 Turn the box shape right sides out as shown.

11 To attach the lid, place it right sides together against one side of the box. Oversew the edges together.

12 Sew up the next side of the box. This time you will have to work right sides out, so make tiny stitches as they will show.

13 Sew up the next side in the same way, then leave the last side open for stuffing, leaving the needle attached. Stuff the pin cushion firmly with kapok, pushing it into the corners.

14 Sew up the final edge with tiny oversewing stitches.

15 Snip the tacking stitches with sharp scissors and pull them out.

What next?

You can make these colourful pin cushions in so many ways. Be inventive with your fabric choices. Stripes can make exciting, almost 3D patterns!

Beautiful Belt

You will need

- Card or plastic for templates
- Ballpoint pen or soft pencil
- Fabric scraps, striped and plain
- Scissors
- Sewing machine
- Needles and threads to match fabrics
- Iron
- Lining fabric, 10 x 89cm (4 x 35in)
- Two strips of craft interfacing, 8 x 87cm (3⅛ x 34¼in)
- Imitation suede lacing
- Pins

This versatile belt will brighten up any outfit, whether just jeans or a dress.

The patterns for the Beautiful Belt, shown half actual size. You will need to enlarge them to 200% on a photocopier.

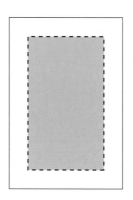

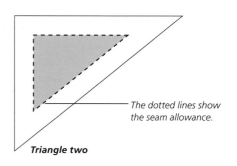

The dotted lines show the seam allowance.

Triangle two

Triangle one

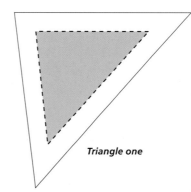

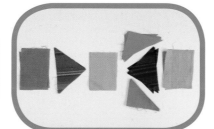

I Photocopy the patterns, draw round them on card and cut them out to make templates. Draw round the templates on your fabric.

2 Cut out three rectangles each in three different colours of fabric; four each of triangle 1 in two different striped fabrics and eight each of triangle two in two colours, as shown.

3 Take a triangle 1 in the first striped fabric and lay a triangle 2 on top as shown, right sides together, with an equal overhang at each end.

4 Thread up the sewing machine with matching thread in the top and the bobbin and sew along the edge with a 1cm (3/8in) seam allowance.

5 Sew all the striped triangle 1 shapes to the pink triangle 2 shapes in the same way.

6 Sew the orange triangles to the left-hand sides of the other striped triangle 1 shapes. Press the seams open with your fingers and carefully iron them flat.

7 Each triangle 1 now needs to have the opposite coloured triangle 2 on its other side. Place each triangle 2 right sides together against the right-hand edge with an equal overhang each side as shown.

8 Sew the second triangles in place by machine, leaving a 1cm (3/8in) seam allowance as before.

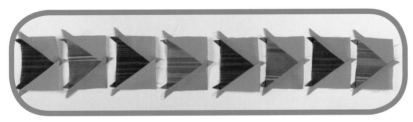

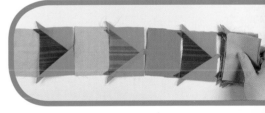

9 Iron all the seams open, then iron all the right sides, and lay out all the patchworked triangles as shown.

10 Place the plain rectangles between the patchworked triangles in sequence. Stack all the pieces in sequence.

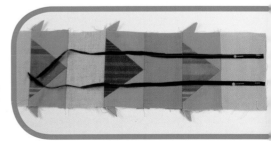

11 Machine sew the rectangles to the patchworked triangles with a 1cm (3/8in) seam allowance. Iron the seams open and iron the front as well.

12 Cut out a lining to fit the belt, 10 x 89cm (4 x 35in). Take the two strips of craft interfacing, place them sticky side down on the back of the belt and on the lining, and iron them on.

13 Take four pieces of imitation suede lacing, each 33cm (13in) long and pin them on either end of the front of the belt, as shown.

14 Place the lining and the belt right sides next to each other and pin them together.

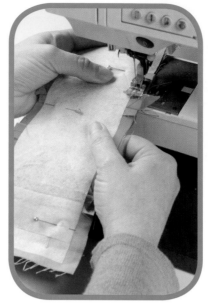

15 Start one third of the way down a long side and machine sew along the edge of the craft interfacing. Sew all round the edge, leaving one third open in the middle of the edge you started with. Turn corners as shown on page 96.

16 Take out the pins and snip off the corners and the overhanging bits of triangles.

TOP TIP!

Remember that snipping the corners carefully will give the belt a professional finish.

17 Turn the belt right sides out and push the corners out using closed, blunt scissors.

18 Fold the edges of the gap over the craft interfacing. Iron them down and pin them.

19 Thread a needle with doubled matching thread. Come up from the inside to hide the knot and sew up the gap using ladder stitch (see page 11).

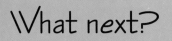

What next?

Try using different patterned fabrics which will make completely different effects depending on how you arrange them. You could also embellish your belt with beads and sequins!

Patchwork Pillow

This wonderfully modern pillow is so simple and quick to make, and can be given as a gift or used to brighten your bedroom!

You will need

Clear plastic and brown paper for templates

Ballpoint pen

Scissors

Five different flowered fabrics and plain and striped fabrics for stalks

Sewing machine and threads to match fabrics

Iron

Pins

Two pieces of backing fabric, each 50 x 22cm (19¾ x 8¾in)

Pillow insert, 48 x 27cm (19 x 10⅝in)

1 Make 8cm (3⅛in) square templates from clear plastic. This means that you can choose good areas of your flowery fabric before drawing round the templates. Cut out sixteen flowered squares from a variety of fabrics. I have used five fabrics.

2 Make stalk templates from brown paper, one 18 x 6cm (7 x 2⅜in) and one 18 x 4cm (7 x 1½in). Draw round the templates and cut out ten narrow stalks and seven wide stalks in four different fabrics.

3 Lay out the squares in two rows in a repeat pattern, and the stalks underneath. Alternate wide and narrow stalks but have narrow ones at either end. This is a chance for you to work out how you want your patchwork pillow to look.

4 Pick up the patchwork pieces one by one and make a stack for each row.

! STAY SAFE
Always ask an adult to help you set up the sewing machine.

5 Take the first two squares from the stack and place them right sides together. Match up the edges carefully. Thread up the sewing machine with matching thread. I have used pale green on the top and in the bobbin. Set the gauge for a 1cm (³⁄₈in) seam allowance and sew along one side to join the squares. Lift the foot, pull out the piece and trim the threads.

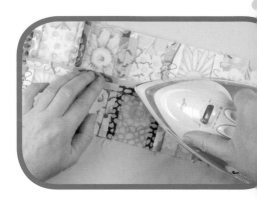

6 Sew together the whole row in this way, then iron the seams open.

7 Sew together the second row of squares in the same way. Then place the first and second rows right sides together, matching up the seams carefully, and machine sew them together with a 1cm (³/₈in) seam allowance.

8 Iron this seam open.

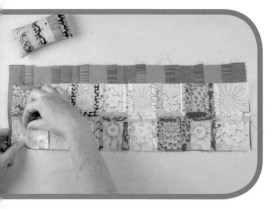

9 Sew the stalks together in the same way. Line up the patchworked stalks and the patchworked squares and place them right sides together. Pin them in place.

10 Machine sew the stalks and the squares together with a 1cm (³/₈in) seam allowance. Make sure the seams are still open back and front, and remove the pins as you go.

11 Iron the new seam open.

TOP TIP!

Ironing the seams flat at each stage will make all the difference to how well the patchwork pieces go together.

12 Iron the front of the piece and trim any edges that need to be evened up.

13 Take a backing piece. Turn over the long edge 1cm (⅜in) and iron it down.

14 Turn the edge over again and iron again. Repeat for the other backing piece.

15 Thread the sewing machine with matching thread in the top and bobbin. Sew along the folded edge close to the fold. Sew both pieces.

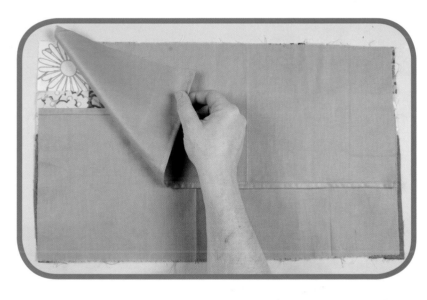

16 Place the pillow case front right side up. Place one backing piece on top with the folded edge upwards, and the second piece on top of that with the folded edge downwards.

17 Pin all the way round the edge of the pillow case.

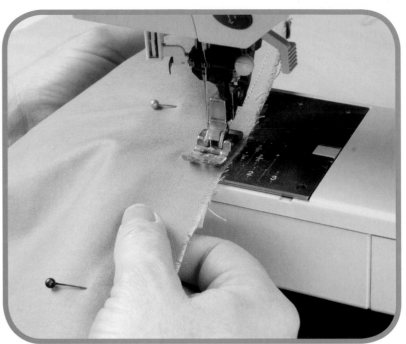

18 Sew all the way round the edges of the pillow case with a 1cm (³⁄₈in) seam allowance. Turn the corners as shown on page 96.

19 Take out the pins. Trim the corners by cutting across them diagonally from each side. Do not cut as far as the stitching.

20 Turn the pillow case right sides out and push out the corners with closed scissors. Put in the pillow insert to complete your patchwork pillow.

What next?

Make covers for pillows you have at home. Fabrics in contrasting colours look great. Try different ways of laying out the patchwork pieces, such as alternating floral and plain fabrics.

Heart Decoration

These decorations will look wonderful at any time of year hanging from a mantelpiece or elsewhere around the home.

You will need

Card or brown paper for templates

Iron

Ballpoint pen or soft pencil

Striped and plain fabric

Scissors

Sewing machine and threads to match and contrast with fabrics

Medium-weight craft interfacing

Pins and needle

Kapok filling

Ribbon, 25cm (10in) long

Two buttons

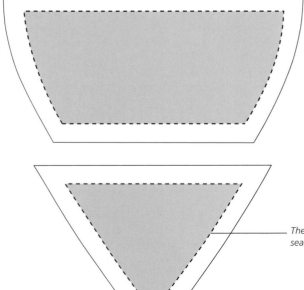

The patterns for the Heart Decoration, shown half actual size. You will need to enlarge them to 200% on a photocopier.

The pattern for the craft interfacing template.

The dotted lines show the seam allowance.

1 Photocopy the patterns, cut out the shapes and draw round them on card or brown paper to make templates. Iron the fabric and draw round the templates on your chosen fabric.

2 Cut out two shapes for the top of the heart and two for the bottom in striped fabric, and two for the middle in plain fabric.

3 Place a top and a middle piece right sides together, matching up the edges carefully.

4 Thread the sewing machine with matching thread in the top and the bobbin. Set the gauge to a 1cm (3/8in) seam allowance and sew the pieces together.

5 Line up the bottom of the heart, right sides together, with the middle.

6 Sew the middle and the bottom together as in step 3.

7 Repeat steps 3 to 6 to make the other side of the heart. Open out the seams at the back of the heart and iron them flat. Iron the front of each piece as well.

8 Make a template from the smaller heart shape and draw round it on craft interfacing.

9 Place the craft interfacing sticky side down on the back of a heart and iron it on. Repeat with the other heart.

10 Choose a contrasting coloured thread (I have used a very pale green) and thread up the sewing machine top. Select an embroidery pattern on your machine (I have used a heart). Sew a line of embroidery either side of each seam.

11 Repeat with the other heart. Place the two embroidered heart pieces right sides together, matching the seams carefully.

12 Pin the pieces together. Place the pins horizontally as shown. Thread up the machine with matching thread top and bottom and change it back to straight stitch. Begin sewing round the edge of the craft interfacing, starting at the bottom of the top section.

13 Sew round the curve to the centre point. Leave the needle in, lift the foot and turn the piece ready to stitch the other curve.

14 Lower the foot again and sew right round the heart, repeating step 13 at the bottom point. Sew to the bottom of the middle section near where you started, leaving the middle section open. Pull the piece out of the machine and snip the threads.

15 Snip diagonally across each side of the bottom point. Do not snip right up to the machine stitching.

16 Make little snips into the curves, but again do not cut as far as the machine stitching. Snip a 'v' shape in towards the centre point.

17 Fold back the edges around the opening you have left in the middle section.

18 Thread a needle with a single tacking thread and do running stitch along each folded back piece to hold them in place. Do not sew up the gap.

19 Turn the heart right sides out and push out the point with closed scissors. Stroke all the seams with the closed scissors.

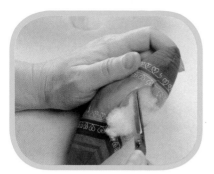

20 Stuff kapok into the curves and the point first, then fill the heart a handful at a time.

21 Sew up the gap using ladder stitch (see page 97). Thread a needle with doubled, matching thread, knot the end and come up through the machine stitching. Make a stitch along the fold on one side.

22 Pull through and make a stitch along the fold on the other side. Do not pull the thread too tight or the heart will be puckered. Continue until you have sewn up the gap.

23 To fasten off, sew over the two sides several times in the same place.

24 Take the needle down and out into the front of the heart to hide the tail of thread inside. Trim very closely. Take out the tacking stitches.

25 Take 25cm (10in) of ribbon and cut diagonally across each end.

26 Knot the end of a matching doubled thread and come up between the curves of the heart. Make a couple of stitches through both sides. Fold the ribbon in half and take the needle through the ribbon ends.

27 Do a couple of stitches through the heart and the ribbon ends to hold the ribbon in place. Take two buttons. Go through a button and back though the heart and ribbon, then through the other button on the other side. Repeat several times.

28 To fasten off, wrap the thread around the base of a button four times. Go down under the button and come up in the middle of the work to conceal the thread ends.

29 Pull through and snip the thread ends.

What next?

Try different shapes, like diamonds or triangles. You could also decorate your shapes with hand embroidery, beads or sequins.

Crazy Bird

This colourful bird can be made in many sizes; in fact you could make a whole family!

You will need

Card or brown paper for templates

Ballpoint pen or soft pencil

Fabric scraps, patterned and plain

Scissors

Medium-weight craft interfacing and iron

Needle, tacking thread and threads to match the fabrics

Sewing machine

Pins

Two 3cm (1¼in) diameter circles of felt and two buttons for the eyes

Kapok filling

The patterns for the Crazy Bird, shown half actual size. You will need to enlarge them to 200% on a photocopier.

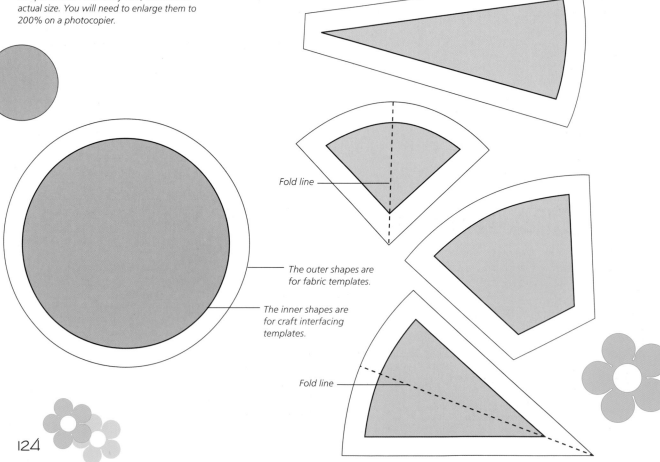

Fold line

The outer shapes are for fabric templates.

The inner shapes are for craft interfacing templates.

Fold line

1 Make a small and a large template for each shape using card or brown paper. Use the larger ones to cut out: two body pieces each in eight different fabrics; one wing in each of two fabrics; two leg pieces in one fabric; two tail pieces in one fabric and one piece for the beak.

2 Use the smaller templates to cut out a craft interfacing shape for each of the pieces in step 1.

3 Place the craft interfacing pieces sticky side down on the backs of the fabric pieces and iron them down.

4 Take a body piece and fold back the fabric edge over the craft interfacing. Fold carefully so that you retain the shape of the curved edge. Thread a needle with a single tacking thread and knot the end. Tack round all the folded down edges.

5 Repeat for all the body pieces. Place two pieces right sides together. Thread the needle with matching thread and knot the end. Sew the pieces together along a long edge with neat oversewing (see page 97).

6 Sew together eight different body parts in this way, then sew together the other eight in the same order to make the other side of the bird. Snip and pull out the tacking stitches you made in step 4.

7 Fold down the edges of each wing piece as in step 4 and tack round them, keeping a neat curve.

8 Thread the needle with a matching thread. Place the wing pieces wrong sides together and use matching thread to oversew around the edges, leaving a 6cm (2½in) gap.

9 Fold back the edges, tack and sew the tail in the same way, wrong sides together. Snip the knots of the wing and tail pieces and take out the tacking stitches.

10 Fold back and tack the straight edges of the beak and leg pieces. Fold the beak piece in half, bringing the straight edges together. Oversew the straight edges together with matching thread. Do not sew up the curve. Repeat for the two legs.

1 1 Place the two sides of the bird's body right sides together, matching the seams. Machine sew along the straight edge with a 1cm (⅜in) seam allowance and matching thread.

1 2 Iron the piece.

1 3 Place the wing circle centrally over the body piece, with half of it either side of the seam. Machine sew it in place.

1 4 Pin and tack the beak, legs and tail in place as shown.

1 5 Ladder stitch the pieces in place (see page 97).

1 6 Place the eye next to the beak. Thread a needle with contrasting thread, come up from the back through the eye and the button, go back down and repeat several times.

1 7 Fasten off at the back by oversewing several stitches on top of one another.

1 8 Sew on another eye on the other side of the bird's central seam.

1 9 Fold the bird in half, matching the seams, and begin to ladder stitch around the edge, starting at the tail end.

2 0 When you reach a leg, ladder stitch along the unsewn side to secure it.

2 1 Sew past the second leg in the same way, then stop and fasten off. Start again at the head end and ladder stitch the beak in the same way as the legs.

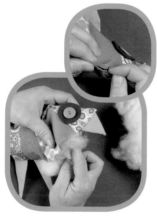

2 2 Leave an opening of 8cm (3¼in). Stuff the bird with kapok filling, then use ladder stitch to close the opening. Remove all the tacking stitches.

What next?

Make a bigger bird as a crazy pillow for your room, or choose brighter fabrics and add sequins for an even crazier, more exotic bird.

Zigzag Bag

This original bag will look great over your shoulder. You could choose fabrics so that it goes with your favourite outfit.

You will need

Brown paper for templates

Ballpoint pen or soft pencil

Scissors

Light, dark, blue and red plain upholstery or thicker cotton fabrics

Pins

Sewing machine and threads to match fabrics

Iron

Pompom fringe

Lining fabric, 1m x 40cm (39½ x 15¾in)

Fabric for handle, 76 x 8cm (30 x 3¼in)

Two large buttons

Needle and tacking thread

The patterns for the Zigzag Bag shown half actual size. You will need to enlarge them to 200% on a photocopier.

The dotted lines show the seam allowance.

1 Make templates from the larger shapes and use them to cut out fabric shapes.

2 Cut out six large triangles in a dark colour and four in a contrasting light colour. Cut out six rectangles in pale blue and six in red.

3 Line up a light and a dark triangle as shown, with an equal overhang at each end.

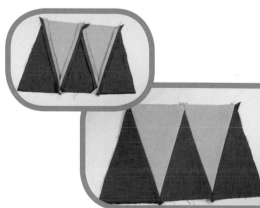

5 Thread up the machine with matching thread top and bottom. With a 1cm (⅜in) seam allowance, sew across the long edge.

4 Pin the pieces together as shown.

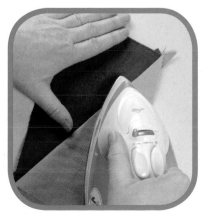

6 Open up the seam and iron it flat.

7 Iron the front of the piece as well.

8 Sew the other triangles to these first two in the same way to complete one side of the bag. Repeat steps 3 to 8 to make the other side.

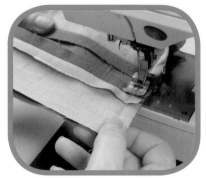

9 Sew together three rectangles, long side to long side in the sequence blue–red–blue. Then sew together the other three in the sequence red–blue–red. Line up the edges carefully and iron the seams flat after you have sewn each one.

10 Put the two sets of three right sides together and match up the seams carefully. Machine sew them together along the shorter edge.

11 Iron the seam flat.

12 Iron the right sides as well. This completes one side of the bag's top section. Repeat steps 9 to 11 to make the other side of the bag top.

13 Put a top section right sides together with a bottom section of the bag. Match up the seams and pin.

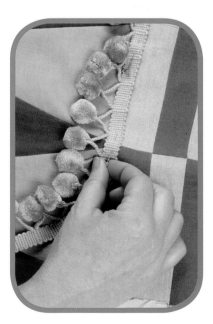

14 Set the machine to a 1cm (3/8in) seam allowance and sew the top to the bottom section.

15 Iron the seam open, then iron the front as well. Repeat steps 13 to 15 to make the other side of the bag.

16 Pin the pompom fringe along the seam joining the top and bottom sections of the bag.

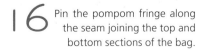

17 Thread up the sewing machine with matching thread and sew the fringe on to the seam with one row of stitching. Pull out the pins as you go. Repeat for the other side of the bag.

18 Draw round one side of the bag on the lining fabric and cut out the shape. Repeat to make the other side of the lining.

19 Place a lining piece over a bag piece, right sides together and pin in place.

20 Thread up the machine with a top thread to match and sew across the top edges to attach the lining to the bag. Repeat for the other side of the bag. Open out and iron the seams.

21 Place the bag front and back right sides together, carefully lining up the seams, and pin.

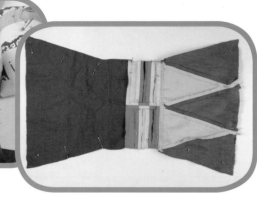

The bag front and back, with linings attached, pinned together.

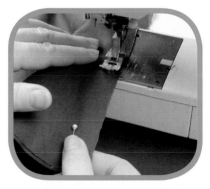

22 Begin sewing on the end of the linings, 12cm (4¾in) from the corner. Turn the corners as shown on page 96.

23 Sew all the way round the bag and lining, leaving a 14cm (5½in) gap in the end of the lining. Make sure that the opened seams remain flat as you sew over them, and be careful not to trap the pompoms in the stitching.

24 Trim across all four corners to make the shape neater when the bag is right sides out.

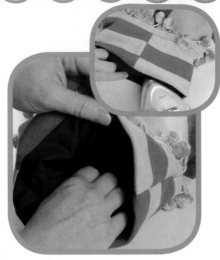

25 Pull the bag through the gap in the opening. Push out all the corners with closed scissors.

26 Iron the opening flat and machine sew across the opening, close to the folded edge.

27 Push the lining inside the bag. Iron the bag, especially at the top where the lining is attached.

28 Take the fabric for the handle. Fold in 7mm (½in) all the way round and iron it in place. Thread a needle with a single thread, knot the end and tack round the edges.

29 Fold the handle in half lengthwise, iron it flat, then pin it in place.

30 Thread up the machine with matching thread and set the gauge to 3mm (¹/₈in). Sew along the end, the long edge and the other end, turning the corners as on page 96.

31 Thread a needle with matching thread. Place the handle end over the bag's side seam, centred 3cm (1¼in) from the top. Place a button on top. Come up from the inside of the bag and go through the handle and button, then go back down through the handle and button. Continue in this way, sewing the handle and button to the bag.

32 Fasten off by sewing several stitches on top of one another in the lining inside the bag. Repeat the other side of the bag to complete the attaching of the handle.

What next?

Make the same bag with flowery and striped fabrics. You could also try making a miniature bag for parties and add some sparkle with beads and sequins.

QUILTING

Miriam Edwards

Quilting is the art of sewing together three layers: backing, padding and then top fabric. You make a 'quilt sandwich' and then join the layers together with stitches or with ties, buttons or beads.

Quilting began in Asia before the first century AD. Europeans discovered it around 1099 when Christian crusaders went to fight the Turks in the Middle East, and saw that they were wearing lightweight quilted armour.

In Europe in the Middle Ages, people wore quilted clothes and used lap quilts to keep out the cold. In the rich houses and castles, large wall hangings helped to keep in the heat.

FUNKY FACT!

In the Middle Ages, soldiers wore quilted clothes under their armour to stop the metal from rubbing their skin.

During the 1500s, quilts were made using fine silks from the East. Quilting remained especially popular in the north of England and Wales. In the north of England, miners' wives would sew for an extra income. The patterns were handed down from mother to daughter. In Wales the quilter was often a single lady who would travel from farm to farm.

When pioneers left England for America, they took the craft with them, and it continued to develop. Small pieces of cloth were sewn together to form a patchwork block. When enough blocks had been made, the pioneer women would meet to sew them together and quilt them.

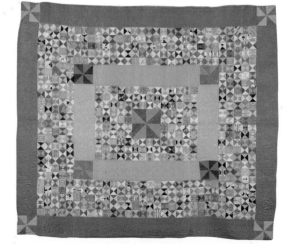

A patchwork quilt from the 1760s.

I have always enjoyed sewing. My mother, aunts and even my grandfather all sewed so as a child I was always surrounded by lovely colourful fabrics and textures. My mother taught me to sew clothes for my dolls, myself and later my own children. I joined a class and soon became addicted to quilting and patchwork. Later I was asked to start teaching children to sew and quilt, which has been a wonderful experience.

I hope you will enjoy the projects in this section twice over: once when you are making them and again when you see the lovely results!

Quilting techniques

☀ Making a quilt sandwich

Place the backing fabric face down on the table, then the wadding on top of that, then the top fabric right side up on top. This forms a quilt sandwich. This is either spray glued together, as in the Cat Wall Hanging, or tacked with large stitches, or pinned with safety pins so that it stays firm while you sew the quilt together.

A quilt sandwich showing (left to right) the top fabric, wadding and backing fabric.

☀ Starting and finishing running stitch

Running stitch is used to sew the layers of the quilt together.

1 Thread your needle as shown.

2 Knot the end of the thread and put the needle through from the back to the front of the fabric.

3 Pull the thread through from the back. Pick up several running stitches at once on the needle.

4 Pull the thread through to show the running stitches. Continue to the end of the row.

5 Put the needle through to the back. Put the needle through a stitch as shown, but not through the fabric.

6 Go through the next stitch in the other direction.

7 Cut off the end of the thread. The thread is now secured at the back.

✳ Overstitch

This is used for sewing two edges together, as in the Sashiko Bag on pages 152–157.

1 Knot the end of the thread. About 1cm (³∕₈in) from where you want to start, come up from the back to the front of the front fabric only. Pull through to bury the knot between the edges.

2 Go in from the back and out to the front where you came out before. Pull the thread through.

3 First you need to secure the beginning of the stitching. Do three diagonal stitches towards the left-hand side as shown.

4 Cross over the first three stitches with three more diagonal stitches towards the right.

5 Continue stitching to sew the edges together. Then go back over two stitches towards the left to secure the end of the stitching.

6 Trim the end of the thread.

✳ Slip stitch

This stitch is used to sew hems. You will need slip stitch to attach the handles on the Sashiko Bag.

1 Tie a knot. Make a little stitch in the backing fabric.

2 Pull the thread through. Fold the hem under as shown. Take up a bit of the edge of the hem.

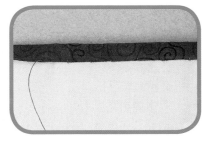

3 Pull through. Underneath the hem, take up a tiny bit of the backing fabric and go into the hem again. Continue as shown.

☀ Tie and buttons

This technique can be used to hold your quilt together, either with running stitches or instead of them. It makes patterns and designs on your quilt, as on the Cat Wall Hanging.

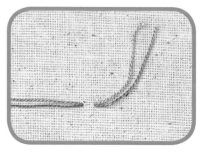

1 Double the thread. Go down and come up again, leaving a tail.

2 Go down and come up again in the same holes as before.

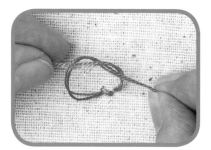

3 Pull the needle through, trim the end to match the tail and tie a knot, right over left.

4 Pull the knot tight and tie another knot, this time left over right.

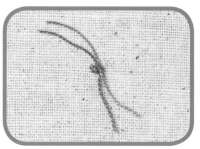

5 Pull the second knot tight and trim the ends.

☀ Adding buttons

To add a button, the steps are the same, but with a button in place as shown.

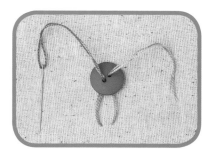

1 Go down and up through the holes in the button.

2 Do steps 2 to 4 as before, but with the button in place.

Glove stitch

This stitch is a strong, decorative way of joining together two raw edges of felt or fabric. It is an alternative to blanket stitch.

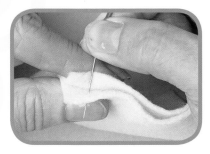

1 Knot the end. Work from left to right. As for overstitch, come up from the back to the front of the front fabric only. This will hide the knot.

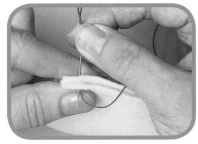

2 Next go from the back through both back and front fabrics.

3 Pull the thread through. Go diagonally 1.3cm (½in) along to the right and go through the back and front fabrics again.

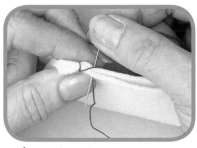

4 Go through once again to finish the stitch.

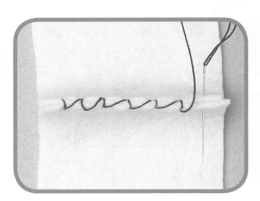

A row of glove stitch worked.

Blanket stitch

This is a way of edging a raw edge of wool or fabric, as on a blanket. I have used it as a decorative way of attaching flowers in the Cat Wall Hanging.

1 Come up at the bottom left and make a stitch going downwards.

2 Pull the thread through, then hold it down with your thumb as shown. Make another stitch downwards.

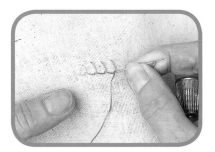

3 Pull through and continue to stitch in the same way. To finish off, take the needle through to the back just underneath the last loop.

Notebook Cover

A5 notebook

Pale pink felt, 45.7cm (18in) square

Purple felt, 25.5cm (10in) square

Cream felt, 12.7cm (5in) square

Scraps of yellow, bright pink, blue and green felt for flowers

Sheer voile, 15.2cm (6in) square

Pins, needles and fabric scissors

Thick purple thread

Thick, variegated pink/ purple crochet cotton

Cotton sewing thread in yellow and black

Three flower buttons

Card, 10cm (4in) square

A4 card for templates

Washable felt tip pen

Shadow quilting is a very old technique, dating back to the 1700s. It is believed to have come from India. It is a way of attaching small pieces of fabric to a background when the pieces are too small to sew. You sew a piece of see-through fabric over the pieces to hold them in place. This tones down the colours of the pieces of fabric like a shadow and creates a soft, dreamy effect.

The pattern for the Notebook Cover, shown full size. Photocopy the design and tape the photocopy to a sheet of card. Cut round the shapes to make card templates of the flowers and stalks.

1 Take scraps of yellow, bright pink, blue and green felt. Hold a flower template on to a piece of felt and cut round it. Cut round the stalk templates on dark green felt.

2 Pin the pieces in place on the cream felt. Pin from the back, as this stops your thread from becoming caught in the pins.

3 Place the voile square over the felt square and pin it in place. Thread a needle with yellow cotton and sew around the flower design in running stitch.

4 Cut the pale pink felt to 33 x 23cm (13 x 9in). Take the card square and place it 2.5cm (1in) down and 2.5cm (1in) in from the top right-hand corner. Draw round it using washable felt tip pen.

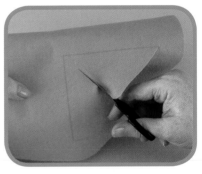

5 Cut out the square. Start in the middle and cut out diagonally to the corners, then cut round the edges.

6 Trim the voile to the edges of the cream felt square.

7 Place the pink felt with the window over the shadow quilted panel and pin it in place.

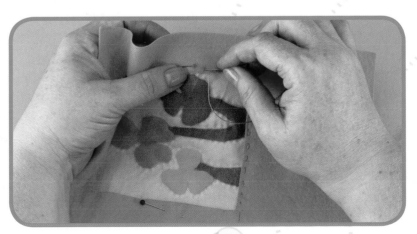

8 Thread a needle with the variegated crochet cotton. Start 3mm ($^1/_8$in) from the edge of the window, at the bottom left-hand corner. Leave a 7.5cm (3in) tail and sew round the window with large running stitches.

9 Leave a 7.5cm (3in) tail at the end and tie the two tails in a

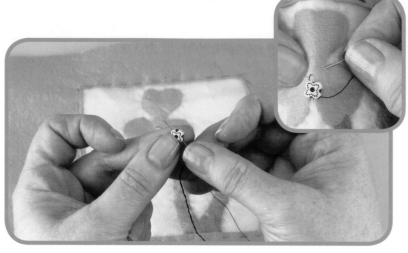

10 Use black thread to sew the buttons to the flower centres. Knot the thread, come up from the back and go through the button. Then go down near to where you came up. Go through all the layers of the shadow quilting. Repeat three times.

11 Secure each button at the back of the quilting with a couple of stitches.

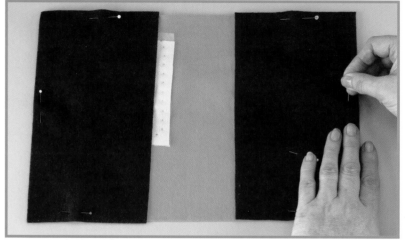

12 Turn over the book cover. Cut two rectangles from the purple felt, each one 12.7 x 23cm (5 x 9in). Pin them in place as shown.

13 Using the thick purple thread, stitch round all four edges of the notebook cover in glove stitch (see page 139).

14 Open your notebook and push the front and back covers into the purple pockets of the notebook cover as shown.

The finished Notebook Cover would look great on your school journal, a sketchbook, address book or diary.

What next?

Book covers make great gifts for your friends. Try different colours and designs, and add beads and sequins.

Fun Phone Pouch

This funky pouch is made using the Japanese folded patchwork technique, which is based on the paper folding art of origami. The pouch has a handy belt attachment and you could use it to hold your glasses, sunglasses or spare change instead of a phone.

1 Use compasses to draw one 11.4cm (4½in) diameter circle and one 12.7cm (5in) circle on card. Cut the circles out.

2 Use a pencil to draw round the 12.7cm (5in) circle on the back of the pink fabric. Draw and cut out four circles.

3 Thread a needle with quilting thread and knot the end. Sew in running stitch round the edge of a circle. Do not cut the thread.

4 Place the pink circle right side down and place the 11.4cm (4½in) card circle in the centre.

5 Pull the thread tight to gather the edges of the pink fabric circle as shown.

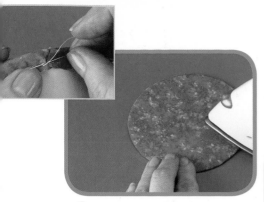

6 Put in a couple of stitches to secure the end, then trim the thread. Make three more circles following steps 3 to 6. Turn the circles over and press them with an iron.

7 Bend the card templates so that you can remove them from the circles.

8 Cut a 7.6cm (3in) square from card. Draw round it on the back of the turquoise fabric four times. Cut out four squares.

9 Cut out four 7.6cm (3in) squares of wadding in the same way. Place a gathered fabric circle wrong side up, then a square of wadding, then a turquoise square right side up, making a small quilt sandwich.

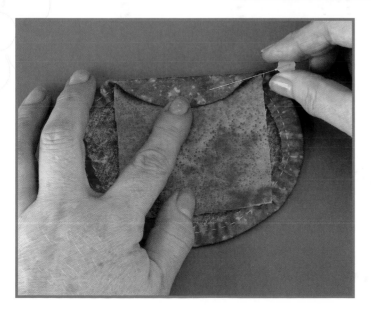

10 Fold the top of the circle down over the top of the square as shown and pin it in place.

145

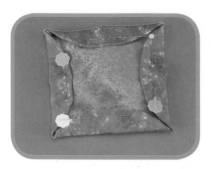

11 Fold and pin the other sides of the circle as shown.

12 Thread the needle with thick variegated thread and knot the end. Come up under the corner of a pink flap to hide the knot.

13 Sew in large running stitches round the edges of the flaps, through all the layers.

14 When you reach the end of one flap, make a stitch over the corner to begin the next flap.

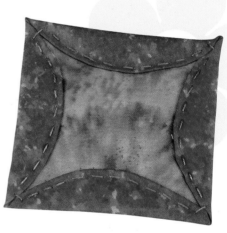

15 The finished square, right side up. Make four squares in the same way, following steps 9 to 14.

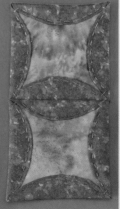

16 Place two of the squares right sides together. Sew them together along one edge, using overstitch (see page 137). This is the front of the phone pouch.

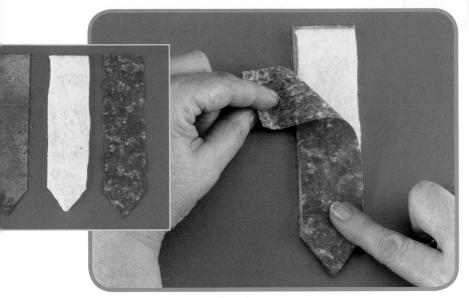

18 Pin the layers together. Thread a needle with the thick variegated thread and knot the end. Go down on the inside of the sandwich and come up on the outside, to hide the knot.

17 Cut rectangles 14.5 x 4cm (5¾ x 1½in) from turquoise fabric, pink fabric and wadding. Trim one end to a point as shown to make tab shapes. Make a quilt sandwich with a turquoise tab shape right side down, a wadding tab shape and a pink tab shape right side up.

19 Sew in large running stitch round the edge of the tab. Make sure your stitches are neat on the turquoise side, since this will show.

20 Lay one quilted square right side up and lay the tab on top, turquoise side down, as shown. The top of the tab should be 6mm (¼in) above the top of the square.

21 Place the last quilted square right side down on top as shown.

22 Pin the top edge and overstitch it (see page 137) using pink cotton.

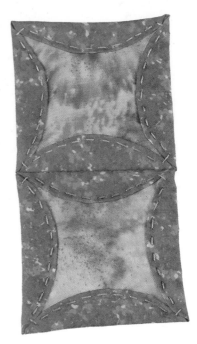

23 Put the back on top of the front, right sides together. Pin the left-hand side. Pin the right-hand side up to the top of the bottom square.

The back and front of the phone pouch should now look like this, right sides up.

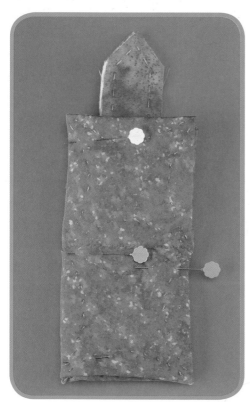

24 Using pink thread, overstitch (see page 137) down the whole left-hand side, across the bottom and up one square only of the right-hand side.

25 Turn the phone pouch right-side out.

26 Fold the tab up and over the top to the front of the phone pouch. Mark with a pin where the tab will need to be fastened to the pouch.

27 Lift the tab and place a second pin in the pouch. This shows where the base of the press stud will go.

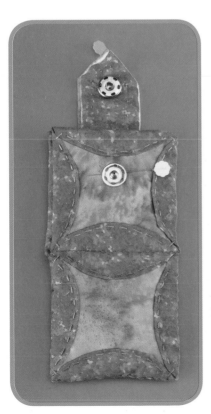

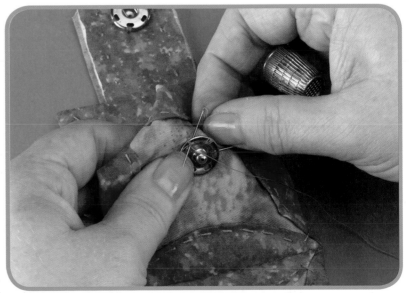

29 Sew on the press stud parts. Use pink thread for the tab, turquoise for the pouch. Hide the knot under the stud and overstitch in and out of the holes.

28 Place the two parts of the press stud as shown.

30 Sew on the flower button. Knot the thread and come up from the back under the button, so that the knot is hidden. Then sew several times through the holes in the button, and finish off with a couple of stitches at the back.

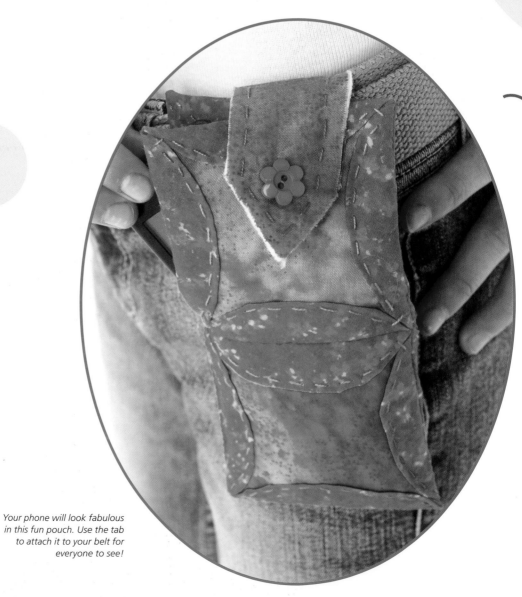

Your phone will look fabulous in this fun pouch. Use the tab to attach it to your belt for everyone to see!

What next?

Why not sew twelve blocks together, making four rows of three, and use it as a lovely make-up bag. You could even make a clutch bag.

Sashiko Bag

You will need

- Two 32cm (12½in) square pieces of blue fabric for the bag lining
- One 32cm (12½in) square of calico
- Two 32cm (12½in) squares of navy cotton fabric
- Handles of your choice
- Thick, variegated thread in blue and orange shades
- Navy thread
- Chalk marker
- Pencil
- No. 7 embroidery needle
- Scissors and pins
- Sticky tape
- Sewing machine

Sashiko means 'little stabs' or running stitch. In Japan in the early 1900s, the wives of farmers and fishermen used to make them warm, protective clothes by sewing together layers of cloth. Later, white thread was used on dark blue, indigo-dyed cloth, in many different patterns. Sashiko was used to sew firemen's protective coats. The patterns were worn on the inside for fighting fires, and on the outside for parades. This pattern is called *seigaiha* or 'waves'.

The pattern for the Sashiko Bag, shown half size. Enlarge it to 200 per cent on a photocopier.

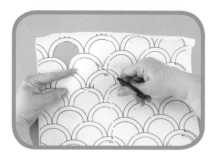

1 Photocopy and enlarge the pattern, then cut out the insides of the wave shapes as shown.

2 Tape the pattern to a navy cotton square. Draw round the pattern with the chalk marker.

3 Place the patterned navy piece on top of the calico square.

4 Pin the navy fabric to the calico. Thread a needle with the thick orange variegated thread and knot the end. Leaving the knot at the back, come up at the bottom right-hand side of the pattern. Begin stitching the design in running stitch.

5 When you come to the bottom of a wave shape, go through to the back and come up as shown to begin the next wave shape along.

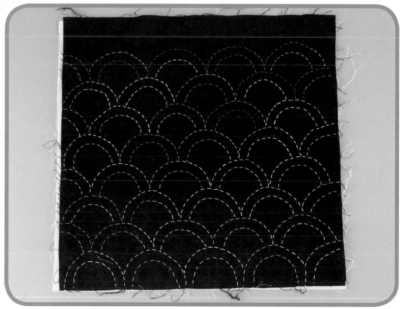

6 Continue stitching the waves from right to left. Stitch all the orange waves first, then thread the needle with the thick variegated blue thread and stitch the blue waves. Remove the pins.

STAY SAFE
Always ask an adult to help you set up the sewing machine.

7 Place the stitched navy square right side up on the table. Place a blue lining square on top, right side down. Pin it in place.

8 Using a sewing machine, begin sewing 10cm (4in) from the top right-hand corner. Sew down to the bottom right-hand corner and sew round the corner.

TOP TIP!
If you sew rounded corners, as I have here, the bag will end up nice and square when you turn it right sides out.

9 Sew along the bottom and up the second side, stopping 10cm (4in) from the top. Take out the pins.

10 Trim round the corners using fabric scissors. Then turn the bag front right sides out.

11 Place the navy square for the bag back on the table, and the blue lining square on top, right side down.

12 Use the sewing machine to sew the back exactly as you did the front: start 10cm (4in) from the top, sew down the side, along the bottom and up the other side to 10cm (4in) from the top. Trim the corners.

13 Turn the bag back right sides out. Place the bag front on top of the bag back, right sides together.

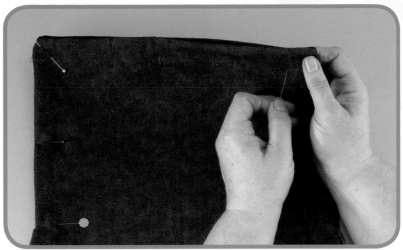

14 Carefully pin together the machine-stitched edges of the bag, leaving the top 10cm (4in) unpinned.

15 Use the sewing machine to sew the back and front of the bag together, leaving the top 10cm (4in) unstitched on both sides as before.

16 Turn the bag right sides out.

17 Take the open edges at the top of the bag, and fold them in 6mm (¼in). Pin them.

18 Overstitch (see page 137) along the edge of the bag front, starting at the top.

19 Continue stitching down to where the front and back of the bag meet, and up to the top part of the bag back.

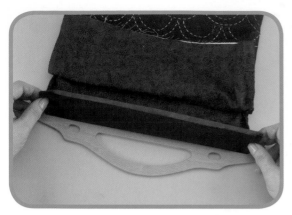

20 Place the back right side up and thread the back through the slot in the handle.

21 Fold the top edge of the bag back in 6mm (¼in).

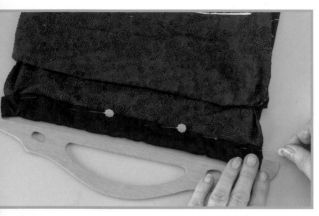

22 Fold the top down over the base of the handle and pin it in place as shown.

23 Slip stitch (see page 137) the folded-over edge to the bag back. Repeat steps 20 to 23 to attach the handle to the bag front.

This Japanese quilting technique makes a really unusual, stylish bag.

What next?

Make a sashiko hipster belt using bright thread and decorate the ends with tassels to match.

Beady Bag

You will need

- Two pieces of calico, 23 x 25.5cm (9 x 10in)
- Two pieces of top fabric, 23 x 28cm (9 x 11in)
- Two pieces of lining fabric, 23 x 30.5cm (9 x 12in)
- Extra lining fabric for the strap, 91.5 x 6.5cm (36 x 2½in)
- Two pieces of wadding, 23 x 25.5cm (9 x 10in)
- Wadding for the strap, 91.5 x 2.5cm (36 x 1in)
- Dark green quilting thread
- Thick orange thread
- Ordinary sewing cotton to match fabric
- Fine needle, pins and safety pins
- Seed beads
- Two buttons
- Sewing machine
- Iron

For this bright and beautiful beaded bag, choose a fabric you really like, with designs you can quilt around. Then cut out pieces for the front and back that show your favourite designs. This is called 'fussy cutting'. Some of the lining fabric will show, so choose something that will look good with your main fabric.

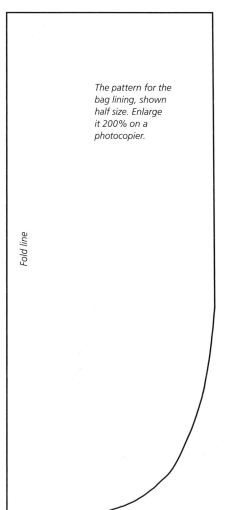

The pattern for the bag lining, shown half size. Enlarge it 200% on a photocopier.

Fold line

The pattern for the top fabric, wadding and backing fabric. The pattern is shown half size. Enlarge it 200% on a photocopier.

Fold line

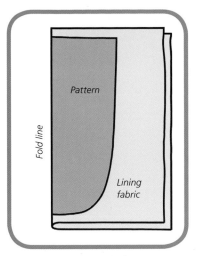

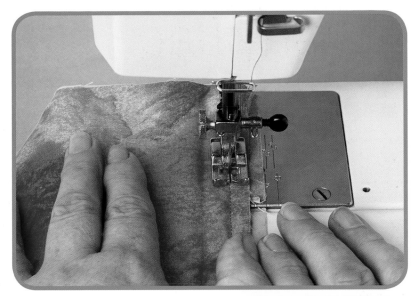

1   Cut out the enlarged patterns. Fold a piece of lining fabric in half and pin the lining pattern on top, with the edge marked 'fold' on the fold of the fabric. Draw round the pattern and cut out the shape. Repeat to make a second lining shape.

2   Use the top fabric pattern to cut out the top fabric, calico backing and wadding shapes; two of each for the front and back of the bag. Place a lining piece and a top fabric piece right sides together and use a sewing machine to sew them together, 6mm (¼in) in from the straight edges. Repeat for the back of the bag.

! **STAY SAFE**
Always ask an adult to help you set up the sewing machine.

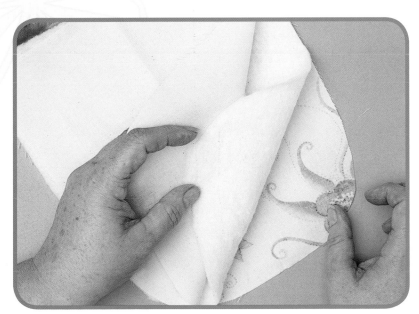

3   Open out the shapes. Make two quilt sandwiches, one for the front and one for the back. Layer the front fabric (right side down), wadding and calico backing shapes as shown.

4   Safety pin the top fabric, wadding and calico backing together.

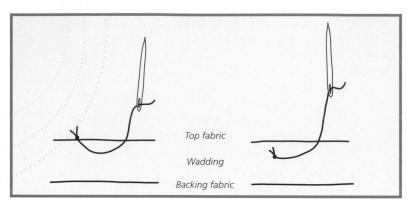

5 Thread your needle and knot the end of the thread. Place the quilt sandwich with the top fabric uppermost. Go down through the top fabric and into the wadding, near to where you want to begin quilting. Come up on the quilting line and gently pull so that the knot pops into the wadding. Now the knot will not appear on the surface.

6 Using quilting thread, sew in running stitch through the three layers around the patterns on the fabric. I sewed round the flowers and birds. Pick up beads on your needle and add them as you go. I added beads for the birds' eyes and for the flower centres.

7 Fold the lining fabric back under the quilted bag front and use an iron to press the edge as shown.

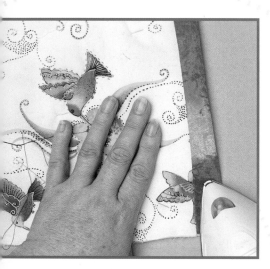

STAY SAFE

Always have an adult with you when you are ironing.

8 Repeat steps 3 to 7 to make the bag back. Take the bag front and open out the lining again. Place the bag front right side up. Open out the lining from the bag back and place it right side down on top of the bag front as shown.

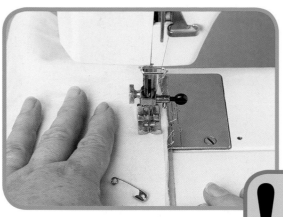

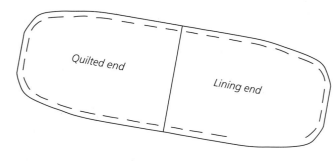

Quilted end

Lining end

STAY SAFE
Always ask an adult
to help you set up
the sewing machine.

9 Thread a sewing machine with ordinary cotton to match the main fabric. Sew right round the full oval shape, both through the quilted front and back and the lining front and back (see the diagram top right). Leave a gap in the lining end.

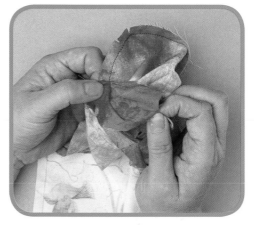

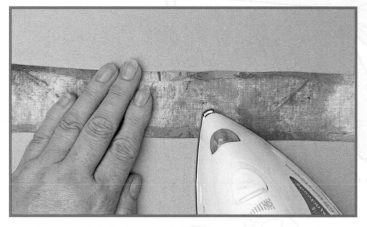

10 Pull the bag and lining through the gap in the lining so that the bag is right sides out.

11 Take the fabric for the strap. Fold in 6mm (¼in) each side and press with an iron.

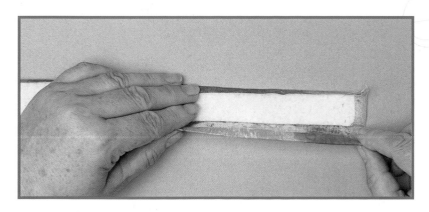

12 Fold the strap in half lengthwise. Fold in 6mm (¼in) at each end and press with the iron again. Place the wadding in the strap as shown. Tuck it under the fold at the end of the strap. Fold up the bottom half of the strap to cover the wadding.

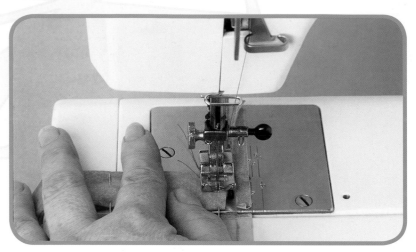

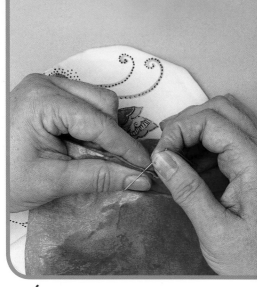

13 Pin all round the edges of the strap and then sew round it with the sewing machine.

14 Slip stitch (see page 11) the gap you left in the bag lining.

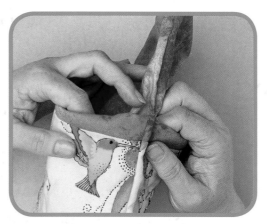

15 Push the lining inside the bag.

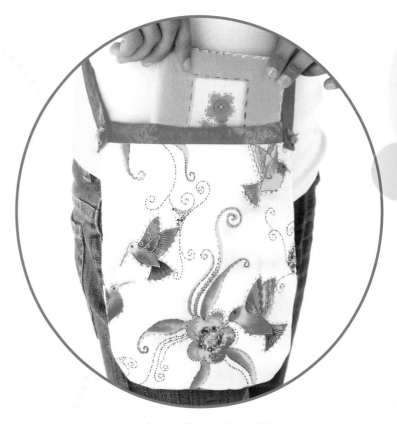

Choose fabulous fabrics and bright little beads for a beautiful Beady Bag.

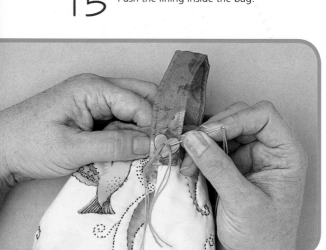

16 Pin the strap to the bag at the side seam. Attach it using a heart-shaped button with doubled thick orange thread and the tie and buttons technique (see page 138).

What next?

Why not make a little bag or purse to clip on to your belt hook?

Cat Wall Hanging

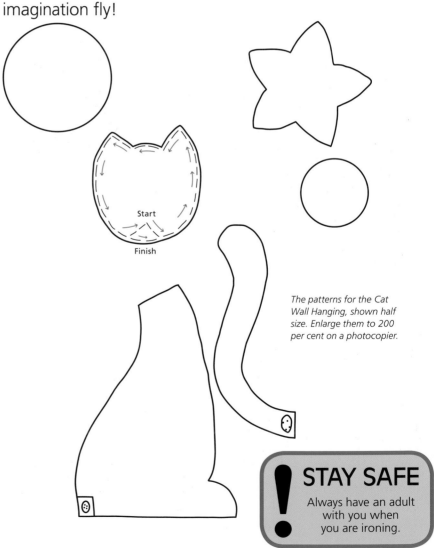

This is a fun project that you could easily make in a day. It uses those precious buttons that people save. This type of quilt is called a 'scruffy' quilt, because it has no binding round the edge, so the rough edges show. You can be really creative with this type of quilt – let your imagination fly!

Start

Finish

The patterns for the Cat Wall Hanging, shown half size. Enlarge them to 200 per cent on a photocopier.

! STAY SAFE
Always have an adult with you when you are ironing.

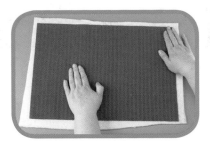

2 Place the wadding on top and smooth it down. Spray the wadding and place the top fabric on top, right side up.

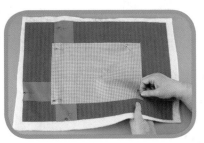

3 Place the pink strips where you want them; they look best off-centre as shown. Place the check fabric on top. Pin everything in place using safety pins.

| Place the backing fabric face down and spray it with fabric adhesive spray. Follow the instructions on the can.

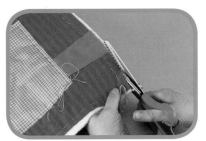

4 Thread a needle with the thick variegated pink thread. Go in at the bottom right-hand corner of the check fabric, leaving a 12cm (4¾in) tail at the end. Sew round the check fabric in large running stitch, 1cm (³⁄₈in) from the edge.

5 Leave a 12cm (4¾in) tail at the end, and tie the two tails in a bow.

6 Sew around the wall hanging 2cm (¾in) from the edge in the same way, using the thick orange/yellow thread. Tie bows wherever you run out of thread. Trim round the edge of the quilt sandwich using pinking shears.

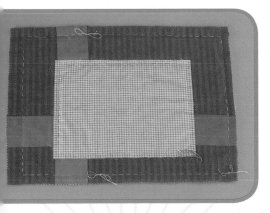

The wall hanging should now look like this.

7 Place a sheet of fusible web, smooth side up over the enlarged patterns. Trace the cat pieces in pencil.

8 Cut roughly round the edges of the cat shapes. Place the fusible web on the beige felt and press with an iron, following the instructions for your fusible web.

9 Cut out the beige shapes, cutting carefully along the lines.

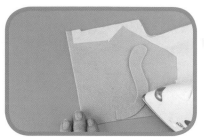

10 Peel off the backing from the tail shape. Place it on another piece of beige felt, fusible web side down. Press with an iron.

11 Cut out the shape so that you have a double thickness felt tail.

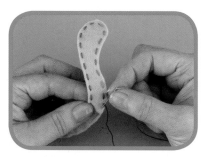

12 Sew round the tail in running stitch using the thick orange/ brown variegated thread.

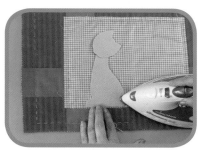

13 Peel off the backing from the head and body shapes of the cat, and place them sticky side down as shown. Press with the iron.

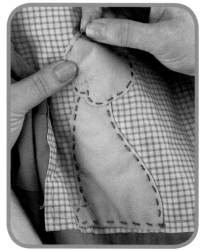

14 Sew round the head and body of the cat in running stitch, using the thick orange/brown thread.

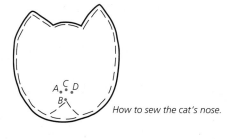

How to sew the cat's nose.

15 To finish the cat's face, you need to sew the nose. See the diagram above. Bring the needle up at A and go down at B.

16 Come up at C and go down at B again.

17 Come up at D and go down again at B.

18 Secure the sewing at the back of the wall hanging with two little stitches through the backing fabric only.

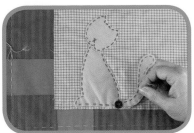

19 Place the cat's tail and the button. Knot the end of the orange/brown thread and come up from the back through the tail and the button. Sew the button on.

20 Draw a 12.7cm (5in) circle on card, using compasses.

21 Draw round the card template on the wrong side of the pink fabric, using pencil.

22 Thread the needle with a long pink thread. Turn the edges of the pink circle in 6mm (¼in) and sew around the circle in running stitch.

23 Pull the thread tight to gather the edges of the circle. Secure with two or three overstitches. This shape is known as a Suffolk puff.

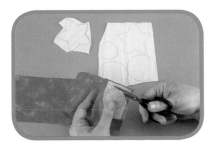

24 Trace two small circles, two large circles and two stars (see page 164) on to the fusible web. Place the shapes on orange fabric. Press with the iron and cut the shapes out.

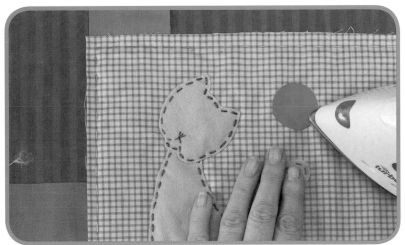

25 Peel off the backing paper from the fusible web. Place the circle above the cat's tail and press it in place with the iron.

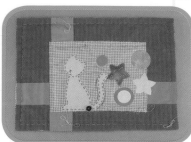

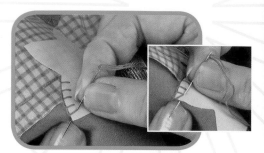

26 Come up from the back and blanket stitch (see page 139) round the edge of the orange circle, using the pale green thread.

27 Attach all the other elements in the same way. Blanket stitch round the purple star and the small yellow circle using matching threads.

28 Sew in blanket stitch round the yellow star. When you reach the corner, go back into the same hole and out to the point. Then go back in the same hole again and out to the edge to turn the corner.

29 Running stitch round the green circle using pink variegated thread.

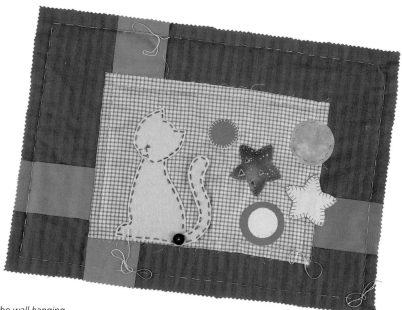

The wall hanging with the shapes attached and stitched.

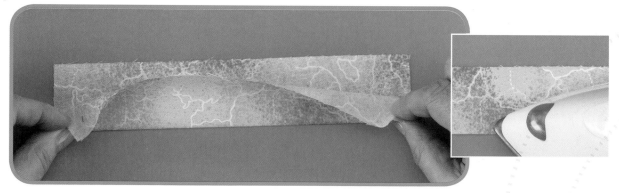

30 Take the strip of yellow fabric for the scruffy flower and fold it in half lengthwise. Press along the fold with the iron.

31 Thread the needle with a long piece of yellow thread and knot the end. Sew in running stitch all along the raw edges. Do not trim the thread at the end.

32 Cut a fringe in the folded strip. Cut every 6mm (¼in), from the folded edge up to 6mm (¼in) from the stitched edge.

33 Pull the thread carefully.

35 Attach the scruffy flower using the tie and buttons technique (see page 138).

34 Join the end of the strip to the beginning with two overstitches (see page 137). This makes the scruffy flower shape.

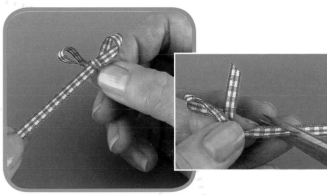

36 Take a long piece of ribbon and tie it in a bow. Trim the ends.

37 Stitch the ribbon to the cat's neck using red thread.

TOP TIP

Practise drawing the cat's face on paper and on scrap felt first.

38 Draw the face on the cat using permanent marker.

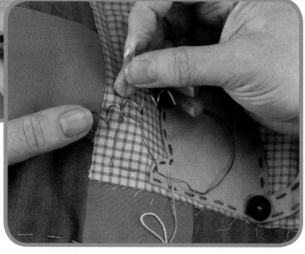

39 Cut three 15cm (6in) lengths of florist wire using old scissors. Holding the end with your thumb, wrap the wire round a pencil to make a spiral. Make three spirals.

40 Thread the needle with turquoise thread and knot the end. Come up from the back and do a few stitches to hold the spiral in place. Repeat for the other two.

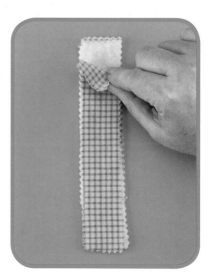

41 Use pinking shears to cut six 21.5 x 3.8cm (8½ x 1½in) check fabric strips for the tabs. Cut three strips of wadding the same size. Make a quilt sandwich with a fabric strip right side down, then a wadding strip, then a fabric strip right side up.

42 Pin the sandwich together. Thread a needle with thick variegated pink thread. Hide the knot inside the sandwich (see page 160).

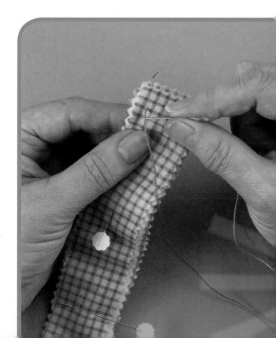

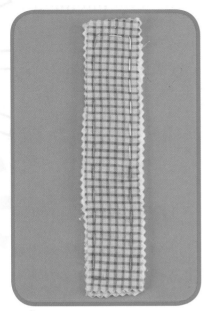

43 Sew in running stitch all round the edge of the tab. Make three tabs following steps 40 to 42.

44 Fold a tab in half and place both ends at the front of the wall hanging, on the sewing line as shown. Pin it in place.

45 Place a large button in front of the tab ends. Thread the needle with doubled thick variegated orange/brown thread. Go in to one of the button's holes leaving a 5cm (2in) tail.

46 Sew around the four holes leaving a 5cm (2in) tail at the end. Tie a double knot and trim. Attach all three tabs in the same way.

47 Use the tie and buttons technique and pink variegated thread to attach the Suffolk puff flower. Attach buttons to the centres of all the other shapes.

Hang the finished wall hanging from the dowelling rod. This project is a great opportunity to raid the fabric scrap bag and delve into the button box for forgotten treasures.

What next?

You can really use your imagination with these wall hangings. Make your favourite pet instead of the cat, and go wild with scruffy flowers!

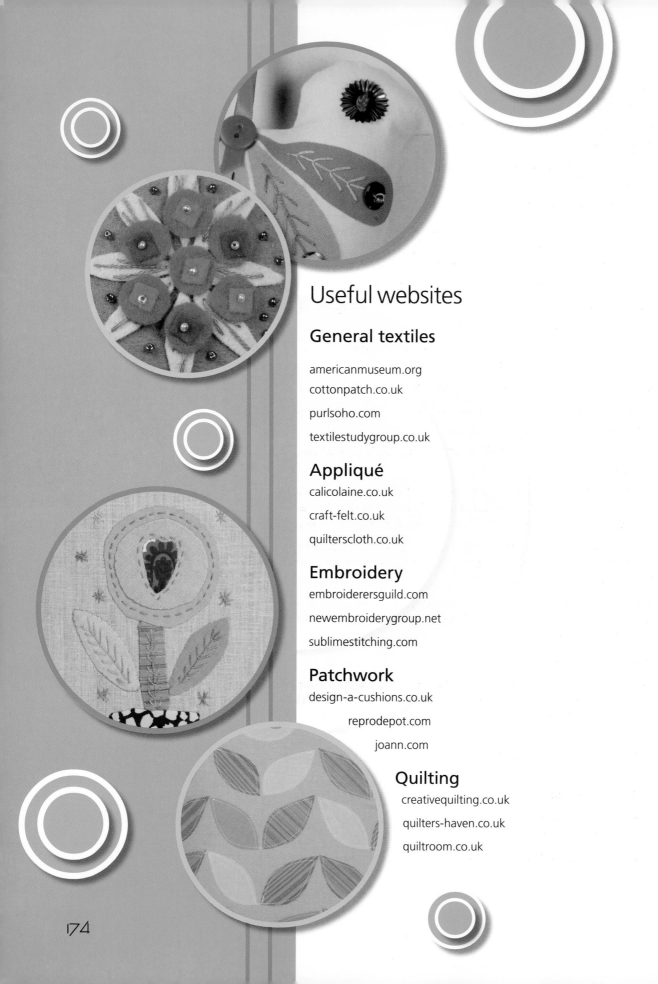

Useful websites

General textiles

americanmuseum.org

cottonpatch.co.uk

purlsoho.com

textilestudygroup.co.uk

Appliqué

calicolaine.co.uk

craft-felt.co.uk

quilterscloth.co.uk

Embroidery

embroiderersguild.com

newembroiderygroup.net

sublimestitching.com

Patchwork

design-a-cushions.co.uk

reprodepot.com

joann.com

Quilting

creativequilting.co.uk

quilters-haven.co.uk

quiltroom.co.uk

Glossary

Appliqué Cutting shapes from one fabric and applying them to the surface of another.

Binding A strip of fabric sewn on to cover the edges of a quilt.

Couch To attach a thick thread to a piece of embroidery by overlaying it with thinner threads.

Crusaders These were fighters from Christian countries who went to fight in the Middle East to get the Holy Land back from Muslim Turks between the eleventh and thirteenth centuries AD.

Embroidery Decorating fabric with needle and thread.

Fusible web This is a type of adhesive for sticking fabrics together. You iron it on and peel off the paper backing.

Patchwork This craft involves sewing together small pieces of fabric into a larger design, which is then often quilted.

Pioneers Settlers in a new land, in this case, America.

Quilting A method of sewing or tying two layers of fabric together with a layer of padding in between.

Sashiko A Japanese style of quilting with running stitch patterns on dark blue fabric.

Seam allowance This is the distance between the cut edges of the fabric and the stitching when you sew two pieces of fabric together. You can set the gauge on your sewing machine for the seam allowance that you want.

Shadow quilting Small pieces of fabric are placed on a backing fabric, with a transparent fabric such as voile on top. You then stitch round the design to attach the layers together.

Shakers A protestant religious group that began in England in 1747 and later set up communities in America. They became well known for their furniture and quilts.

Skein A length of yarn, wound into a coil.

Stranded embroidery thread This is a loosely twisted thread made up of six strands, used for hand embroidery techniques. The strands can be separated so that the thread can be as thick or as thin as you want it for your embroidery.

Translucent Partly see-through.

Variegated thread This has patches of different colours or different shades of one colour.

Wadding The layer of padding that goes on the inside of a quilt sandwich. In the US it is called 'batting'.

Weaving Interlacing threads or strips of fabric at right angles to each other.

Index